Testim<

I love The Business Jet Engine® . . .

or an experienced business owner, this book will re-energise your business planning. It describes the key parts of a business that keep your business flying high, and helps you prioritise what to improve next. It's helped me to significantly transform my own business!

Michael Tyrrell
Simply Beautiful Print

We use The Business Jet Engine® *to great effect. It's a simple but powerful tool that helps us create an aligned strategy across all our branches.*

Stewart Pierce, Financial Director
Parker Building Supplies

The Business Jet Engine® *takes something that could be overwhelming or confusing, and breaks it down into a clear, pragmatic approach. It gives you a simple road map to plan your business, so you focus on what is important and do not waste time on areas that are already good enough.*

Emma Bridger, MD
PeopleLab

There is a real power in a simple diagram. The Business Jet Engine® *makes it easy to talk about all the parts of a business. At any given time, some part of your business will be out of balance. It will be below where you want it to be and* The Business Jet Engine® *allows you to highlight the importance of that area and discuss how to improve it with your team.*

Steve Mainstone, MD
Main Systems

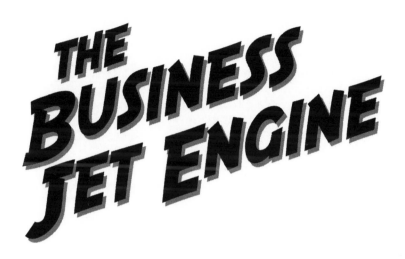

THE BUSINESS JET ENGINE

The Simplest Guide to Boost Your Business

Martin Riley

Martin Riley Publishing
The Studio, Pashley Farm
Bexhill-on-Sea
East Sussex
TN39 5JS
United Kingdom

info@businessjetengine.co.uk

First Edition

ISBN 978-1-9997454-0-0

Typeset in 9/15pt Helvetica Neue Light by Falcon Oast Graphic Art Ltd.
Printed in Great Britain

Cover design: Tony Seddon
Interior design: Falcon Oast Graphic Art Ltd.

www.businessjetengine.co.uk
The Business Jet Engine® is a registered trademark of Martin Riley

Elliot & Isabelle
Jonny, Brooke, Jane & John
Cyndi & Tom
Judith
AJ, Martin L-E, Pring . . .
for your love, friendship – and always being there!

Acknowledgements

There are a vast number of people to whom I am deeply grateful. As always, there are too many to mention, and by mentioning anyone by name, I risk omitting another of equal importance. There are those who played a major part in my lifelong development and those who influenced this book directly. However, I shall do my best to acknowledge my friends and colleagues who I believe have been most instrumental in bringing this book to fruition.

From my first education and subsequent career in design, I need to mention all those who inspired, challenged and guided me; my first tutor John Doyle and fellow students Phil Cook and Jane Eden. Then professionally; Geoff Hollington, John Choong, Fred Bold, Mark Chittenden, George Kasabov, Barry Weaver, Phil Gray, Jon Tremlett and Morag Hutcheon – you all taught me, stretched me, challenged me.

Through my transition from designer to coach, I owe much to Sunil Mistry who shared many of the ups and downs. I owe a huge debt of gratitude to Gil Dove, who shared all his skill and insight, but also challenged every assumption and tested to destruction all I held dear. Stand-out clients who were a particular joy to work with at that time include Ed Bussey, Chris Clayton, Clive Grinyer and Jean Bolwell, who in my earlier coaching days, entrusted me with their challenges and allowed me to hone my skill.

Since then, I have enormous gratitude to all my Sussex clients. In particular I would like to mention Joel and Tom at Switchplane, who are not only my longest standing clients, but have a wicked sense of humour and are a continual pleasure to work with. Of course I should mention Dan Stone for our Business Jet Engine® breakthrough moment. James Bartleet who helped refine the model. In addition, I am indebted to Stewart Drew at the De La Warr Pavillion for our projects and friendship, and Graham Pitts and Stewart Pierce at Parker Building Supplies for our long-term involvement and trust.

My expert contributors to the Fine Tuning section need a very special mention; Graham Seymour, previously of Shopper Anonymous, Doug Edworthy of Edworthy Management Consultants, Chris Clayton of Grey Matters (Europe) Ltd, Clifford Thomas of Business Development Consultancy, Emma Pearce of Pearce Marketing, Shaun Walsh of Business Growth Services, Peter Watters of McPhersons Chartered Accountants – and Antonia Chitty for her editing skill.

In addition, there are so many dear friends, colleagues and advisors who have cheered from the side-lines. Just a few who have helped guide, encourage and support me on this book journey include Mollie Tucker, Natasha De Grunwald, Richard Morecombe, Dan Bradbury, Rick McMunn, Simon Coulson, Jen 'Perks' Tonkin and Inka Hajman. Your encouragement and support has been invaluable!

Through all of this Amanda Wright, Martin Lloydd-Elliot and Martin Pring – I don't have the words for my love for you! To my family; Dad, Mum, John, Jonny, Judith, Elliot and Isabelle, you put up with me through it all . . . what can I say other than you are my world.

And perhaps above all, this book simply would never have reached completion without the skill, care and diligence of my colleague Richard Best who has been instrumental in this project reaching its end. I thank you especially.

With my deepest gratitude, I thank you all. – Martin

Contents

Foreword

I first met Martin at the start of the new millennium. We were both taking a major leap of faith and making significant transitions from our former careers – in Martin's case from product design to leadership coaching and in mine, from the Royal Navy and Foreign Office into the world of entrepreneurship and ecommerce.

We immediately recognised in each other a passion to go beyond the ordinary; a desire to do something worthwhile – and to do so with integrity, while bringing others along with us. So, when Martin contacted me recently to say that he had created a tool to help SME businesses, I was certain it would be worth looking at.

As a serial entrepreneur – and having experienced all the ups and downs that come with growing early stage businesses – I understood the problem that Martin was trying to solve. I could see that he wanted to educate people on the critical (but often overlooked) aspects of running a business, enabling SMEs to sidestep many years of painful trial-and-error learning and plan their next moves armed with knowledge informed by experience.

I learned many of these lessons the hard way, but was fortunate to achieve early success. My first venture was as CMO of *figleaves.com*, where within four years, we had acquired over one million online customers in 66 countries. I then became COO at ZYB, a fast-growth Scandinavian mobile technology firm that was acquired by Vodafone in 2008 for £28.5m. After an unsupported charity trek to the North Pole in the spring of 2010,

I was ready to start Quill, supporting ecommerce businesses with a scalable digital content production service.

In this book, Martin rightfully stresses the importance of competitive advantage. At Quill, our mission is to produce digital content at unparalleled speed and scale, covering more languages and topics than anyone else. We now work for over 170 companies worldwide – and it still feels as though we're just starting out.

In my first career, the Navy taught me great skills around leading and motivating people. Of course, many business problems can be solved through spreadsheets and analysis, but the most challenging issues are often more to do with people. Martin emphasises the importance of hiring and building the best possible teams and I firmly believe in this principle – and that you need to get this right from the start. Your team are the wings on your jet engine and absolutely essential for take-off.

Whatever journey you are on, and whatever level you are flying at, this book will certainly help you on your way. Congratulations on your spirit of adventure. Running a business takes courage and faith – but also the knowledge to avoid pitfalls and accelerate your progress.

I wish you every success in tuning your Business Jet Engine® and flying high.

Ed Bussey
Serial entrepreneur, founder and CEO of Quill
Winner of Great British Entrepreneur of the Year 2015

Section 1

Stuck on the Runway
...is this you?

This is the introduction to the book to help you get the most from it.

Here you will learn:

- Why this book has been written
- How it can help you
- How best to use it to match your own needs

CHAPTER ONE

Why The Business Jet Engine®?

The aim of this chapter is to explain

- What this book is about
- Who it is for
- The purpose of the four sections
- How to use them for maximum effect

Tips

- Check out what is coming up. You will learn faster if you know where this is heading
- Go to the bonus content at www.businessjetengine.co.uk
  - Watch the video animation
  - Print out The Business Jet Engine® diagram in colour
- Skim the contents page at the start of the book
- Read *How to use the book sections* in this chapter
- Read the chapter summaries at the start and end of each chapter
  - The aim of this chapter
  - What you have learned

Actions

- Follow the tips above
- Decide how to best use this book to boost your business

Why Read this Book?

- Are you frantically busy running your business?
- Are you short on time with too much to do?
- Even if your business is doing well, do you feel it could be:
  - Much more efficient?
  - Much less stressful?
  - Much more rewarding?

You may be new to business, or you may have been running one for some time, but do you somehow feel that there is something missing, some clarity, to make it work properly? Or you may be highly experienced but find it hard to get your team to think the same way and willingly work to the same goals?

You may be familiar with the many aspects of business, such as operations, finance, profit, sales, competitive advantage, overheads and customer feedback. You may have read lots of articles and books on the subject. Despite this knowledge, it can be hard to know what to focus on first, to know which parts to improve that will make the biggest difference.

> *This book will help you see your business as a whole, to see the connection between all the major parts, and evaluate what action to take.*

Common business mistakes

One of the biggest mistakes that many businesses make is trying to improve too many elements at once. This leads to a lack of focus and progress resulting in confusion, demotivation and burnout. One of the objectives of this book is to help you focus your priorities for the year ahead. It will help you discover what will make the biggest difference in the long-term.

A business that has focus is more motivated and makes more targeted progress. I have worked with many people over two decades as a leadership trainer and business coach. I've helped business owners put out fires and re-focus so they can grow. I have seen how often they share a similar journey, a common pattern of mistakes, and through this I have discovered the key steps to speed progress.

To help my clients, I have devised a way of putting all these parts together that is far more powerful than a to-do-list of jobs or parts. I put it together as a living, breathing system.

The Business Jet Engine® model

As I watched my clients on their common journey, a metaphor started to appear. I played around with this idea, and developed it further until it grew into The Business Jet Engine® model where all the parts made sense. At last I had a picture, a system, a diagram that clarified everything. This is the system I use today to empower business owners to achieve their goals and dreams.

I use the model to great effect with businesses large and small, from one-man-bands to companies with 300+ staff. Clients who use it wish they had it many years ago. And those more experienced wish they had it earlier to share with their staff.

Who is this Book For?

You may be asking yourself, 'Is this book for me, and will it offer me a return for the time, money and effort I will be putting in?' The simple answer is that this book is designed for you if you are responsible for setting the direction of a business – of any size.

Start-ups and beginners

If you consider yourself a beginner in business, starting up for the first time, this book will help you avoid many of the most common mistakes that businesses make in their first ten years.

Intermediates

If you have been in business a while, this book will serve as a reminder for many principles you already know, but will also highlight gaps in your current knowledge.

Experienced and advanced

If you have a considerable amount of business experience, this book will serve as reminder of principles with which you are already familiar, a checklist for areas you may be omitting, a framework for future planning and a roadmap for working with less experienced team members.

Sometimes with a large business, it is easy to lose sight of business fundamentals. This book will serve as a reminder of the basics that must be correctly in place.

Whatever your level of experience, this book should be of value. This is what I have found with my clients and I truly hope that it will also be of great value to you. I would love your feedback after you have applied the concepts in this book.

Do please email me your feedback at
martin@businessjetengine.co.uk

The Story of Bin Man Dan – finding the value of the model

Bin Man Dan is a great example from the early days of The Business Jet Engine®. It shows the clarity given by the model and why it became such a useful tool.

Dan Stone, owner and founder of Bin Man Dan, was a busy man. His business was waste management and he had four interrelated companies all of which were working flat out.

The first business dealt with household clearance and skip hire. The second, the waste transfer station, collected and sorted their own waste and also provided a dumping and/or sorting station for other local waste companies. A third company offered demolition and ground works. The fourth and final company collected commercial waste for recycling.

When Dan and I first met, business was going well but Dan knew he could achieve so much more.

With four busy companies and a lot of work going through them, it was hard to know what to focus on first. It was easy for Dan to become side-tracked into getting hands-on in any part of a business that was feeling the strain.

Like many business owners, it would have been easy for Dan to think that his way to grow was through more marketing, more sales. 'Let us get more work' is a common cry for growth. Many business gurus claim they can quadruple your business overnight. Their formula is usually more marketing, more sales. It becomes an easy trap to fall into and this could have looked like the answer for Dan.

Instead, Dan and I sat down and took an analytical look at each business. We used The Business Jet Engine® model and applied scores against every part of every business, after which, the picture was surprisingly clear. His best strategy was staring us in the face.

In each of his businesses, operations could be more efficient. We also found that overall the quality of staff had a low score, which is why Dan had to get involved. This left him lacking time to plan. The waste industry requires expensive plant and machinery, requiring significant amounts of capital expenditure to stay up-to-date and Dan was struggling to find time to create a plan for his much-wanted investments.

Having identified the main problem areas, we came up with a focused plan to move the business forward. Operations were the obvious part of the business to fix first. We identified the three most important operational aspects of each business to improve that year.

It was apparent that the operations relied on the quality of staff. The waste industry is a hands-on, dirty environment, at the low end of the pay scale so it can attract indifferent workers. In Dan's business, like many businesses with high staff turnover, people were hired on-the-fly as others moved on. The staff hired were often mates of existing staff who needed work in a hurry, so were similar characters, augmenting Dan's problems.

We came up with a plan to be much more rigorous, only hiring A-players who were interested in remaining long-term, with proper training and the potential of a career path. With action plans in place for improving the quality of staff and efficiency of operations, we turned our attention to Dan to help him find time for proper planning outside the time spent in our sessions. We made sure that time was blocked out in his diary. We mapped out the mission-critical tasks that needed to be achieved in that timeframe, creating clear financial budgets and targets for each business, so that money could be put aside for capital expenditure.

These priorities became the successful focus for that year allowing Dan to take a significant step toward the larger, more profitable business that is JM Waste Management today.

What this Book is and What it is Not

It is not a comprehensive business manual

This is not a comprehensive business textbook or MBA manual. It is not intended to be encyclopaedic or a tome on business best practice. It is a simple guide to business planning. Like having the picture on a jigsaw box, this book gives you that top-level picture so you know where all the pieces fit.

If you want to become more expert in any part of The Business Jet Engine®, there is a wealth of further information available. There are a few suggestions in the bibliography at the end of this book to get you started or you can browse online to find books and courses to suit your need.

Although not comprehensive, what this book will do is highlight simple concepts in each area of your business that can save you years of mistakes. There are tips and tools to improve how you make plans and follow them through. After all, a plan has no value without follow-up action.

The only jet engine that needs no technical knowledge

This book is only loosely based on any true engineering principles. More importantly, it is a story, and a fun idea that anyone is able to embrace. You do not need to be a mechanic.

There are essential parts to a business, just as there are elements that allow an engine to work or a plane to fly. You need to understand these elements well enough to put an initial framework in place that you can build from, diagnose problems when things go wrong, or to train or collaborate with others on your team.

If you are a business owner, or hold a leadership position, then you will need to make strategic decisions that will move your business in the right direction. This model will help you decide exactly what to do.

How Best to Use this Book

Books are great! You can learn so much by reading incredible material, written by experts, that would have been hard to access in any other way. You can scan through sections quickly in advance to gain a rapid insight, before reading a book more thoroughly. You can turn the pages, underline, *mark key phrases*, write in the margin and stick markers against favourite passages. You can refer back-and-forth between the sections of a book at great speed. Which is why I have written this book for you.

That said, it is well worth going straight to the **Free Bonus Content** at *www.businessjetengine.co.uk.* **Watch the free videos and download the tools to help you on your journey.**

Why is that recommended? The story I am going to tell as The Business Jet Engine® model unfolds can be quickly illustrated in a short video. For those of you that like to get the big picture fast, this is the place to go.

As much as I want you to enjoy the story in this book, more importantly I want you to understand the concepts and make great use of these powerful ideas. Start by getting the big picture quickly. The best way to master a subject is by repetition and involvement. So repeat your exposure to this information multiple times, including the videos, and score your own business using the download tool as soon as possible.

Many of us respond well to visual information, rather than just words. Watching the videos introduces an additional learning format to speed the process.

How to use the book sections

This book is divided into four main sections:

Section 1. Stuck on the Runway – is this you?

This is the introduction to the book to help you get the most from it.

Here you will learn:

- Why this book has been written
- How it can help you
- How best to use it to match your own needs

Section 2. Clearance for Takeoff – getting your plans in place

This is the diagnostic and planning section. The first two chapters, 3 & 4 are about diagnosis.

Here you will learn:

- The Business Jet Engine® model
- *How to apply scores to your business at two levels:*
  - **Basic/fast scoring**
  - **Intermediate**

This will show you the journey you are on. More importantly it will help you understand the areas of your business in which you are weakest and what to do next to strengthen them.

Chapters 5 & 6 turn your diagnostic work into meaningful plans for the year ahead.

Here you will learn:

- A quick & simple method of business planning

For the year ahead you will be able to:

- Create a meaningful set of priorities for your own business
- Turn priorities into quarterly goals

- Turn quarterly goals into a one-month task list
- Learn top tips to keep you on track

Section 3: Fine Tuning – *for maximum performance*

This is the section for keeping your Business Jet Engine® tuned so you can climb faster and fly higher. This section will increasingly help you refine and improve your knowledge and business, over time.

Here you will learn:
- Key concepts to strengthen each area of your business
- ***How to apply scores to your business at an advanced level***

These will help you:
- Ensure you have essential frameworks in place for each area of your business
- Guide your own future development and learning

Including more involved concepts of:
- Business planning
- KPIs and measuring and monitoring your progress

Return to this section repeatedly to continually improve your knowledge and the performance of your business. Once you have the basic frameworks in place for each area, you can use the diagnostic questions to direct your development.

Section 4: Flying High – *and keeping it all going*

This section is about taking your knowledge and experience beyond the aims of this book and giving you shortcuts to some of the great information available to speed your learning.

In this section you will learn:

- The importance of a winning mindset
- Key principles of leadership
- The importance of timely reviews

Find guidance on further useful information such as:

- The Business Jet Engine® Online
- Recommended reading

How to use the diagnostic questions and checklists

This book explores the parts of your business at increasing levels of detail.

Section 2. Chapter 4:

- Basic/Fast Scoring Diagnostic Questions
- Intermediate Diagnostic Questions

Section 3. Chapters 7 to 11:

- Advanced Diagnostic Questions

  To use these, score yourself out of 10, where:

  0 = Very weak/poor/no strength or ability
  5 = OK/adequate/just good enough
  10 = Very strong/excellent/no room to improve

This will show you specifically where you are strong or weak in each part of the business.

What you should achieve

By the end of this book you will have a good understanding of:

- What makes a business work
- Where you are weak or strong in your own business
- What you need to improve
- In what order you need to improve those areas

- What you need to learn and develop in the longterm

Most importantly, you will have a clear set of priorities, which you have turned into plans and tasks for the year ahead. This should give you clear focus, and confidence that you are taking your business in the right direction. It will stop you becoming sidetracked in projects that do not really serve your ultimate goals.

What you have learned

- This book is about
  - Better, simplified business planning to give you clarity and focus
- It will show you how:
  - The major parts of a business link to make it work at its best
  - To decide what to improve next
  - To create simple and achievable plans
- The concepts of this book hold true for any size business
- This book is specifically aimed at:
  - Micro, small and medium businesses (SMEs)
  - Business owners and leaders – at all levels of experience
- How to use this book for maximum impact

Tips

- Check out what is coming up. You will learn faster if you know where this is heading
- Go to the bonus content at www.businessjetengine.co.uk
  - Watch the video animation
  - Print out The Business Jet Engine® diagram in colour
- Skim the contents page at the start of the book

- Read *How to use the book sections* in this chapter
- Read the chapter summaries at the start and end of each chapter
  - The aim of this chapter
  - What you have learned

Required actions from this chapter

- Follow the tips
- Decide how to best use this book to boost your business

In the next chapter

- Establish the most important end goal
  - Why are you in business at all?

CHAPTER TWO

Your Own Journey

The aim of this chapter is to clarify:

- Why you are in business
- What you hope to achieve
- If your life and business goals align
- If your level of commitment matches your goals
- My hopes for you and your success

Tips

- Consider your current situation
- Consider what has made you happiest in the past
- Consider what you believe will make you happiest in the future
- Keep business in perspective
  - It supports your life
  - Your business may fill your time, but it isn't life itself!

Actions

- Think about what you *really* want most
- Consider, do your business goals support the life you *really* wish to lead?
- Match your level of commitment to your desired end goal

Why are You in Business?

It is important to know what type of business you are in, what you want to achieve, and whether this supports the life you dream of. If there is a mismatch between any of these, you will be frustrated. If they align well, you will be motivated to succeed. Therefore, you want to get this right at the outset.

Are you in business:

- For fame and/or fortune?
- To pursue your passion?
- Because you want the independence of working for yourself?
- To provide jobs and security for friends and family?
- To make a difference to your community or society?
- For any combination of the above?

What is most true for you and are you clear in your own mind about this?

Common reasons to be in business

There are many benefits and joys to running your own business. I have high-lighted the objectives of common business types, but also the challenges and pitfalls that come with them. By applying the principles in this book you can pre-empt these issues and ensure your business works for you.

Self-employed/one-man-band

The main benefit of running this kind of business is that you have a degree of autonomy because you are working for yourself.

However, if you are the main fee earner, or central to delivery, the business may struggle to operate in your absence. In these situations, rewards can be slim, hours can be long and your stress levels can be high. In addition, if your industry is rife with competition, it can be hard to stand out from the crowd. Because of the time you need to spend generating an income, it can be hard to create a clear plan to move beyond this being similar to just having a job.

Lifestyle business

In this kind of business the owners and possibly staff hope to enjoy a balance between work, friends and family and other interests. The aim is that the business will not be all consuming, but will produce income and profit to support a quality of life beyond work.

Although this is the intention, the reality of running a successful business can be too demanding, which may result in lack of time, money or energy to enjoy life beyond work. The business ends up much like a job as in the sub-section above.

The passion based business

As the name suggests, this is a business based on something you love to do, which you hope to make money from. Often, but not necessarily, you come from the creative or vocational industries such as art, design, music, photography, video, health, yoga, food, fitness etc.

As these tend to be popular options, and therefore plenty of competition, the greatest challenge with this type of business is often being able to attract enough work and charge profitably for what you do. The whole intention with this type of business is to spend your life doing what you love, and in the process, support yourself financially.

It can be easy to underestimate what is required to really generate a comfortable income. In addition, to make any business successful it requires time to plan. If you are busy doing the work you love it can be hard to find time to create plans and ensure sufficient financial success.

The entrepreneurial business

Do you have an idea or concept you are desperate to realise, or do you believe you have spotted a route to make worthwhile sums of money? What typifies this kind of business is the nature of an entrepreneur. As well as being highly driven you are also a perfectionist. You have the skills to get a difficult idea off the ground, to a high standard, and make a rapid impact in your marketplace.

The challenge comes when the business reaches a size where you as the founder cannot be the driving force behind everything. Other people need to run their own departments and make their own strategic decisions. This is the time when you realise you must release control and stop being responsible for everything. You have to trust others to take charge which is entirely different to your original approach. This is called the entre-preneurial trap. A business may develop with a few employees, but because the founder cannot let go, it is unable to grow beyond that size.

Scalable growth business

A scalable business has the potential to grow to a considerable size, and to generate significant turnover and profit. Key ingredients to achieve this kind of growth include an exceptional product or service and high demand from a large pool of repeat customers in a buoyant market.

The challenge here is that it requires systems or processes that can be easily taught and repeated as the business grows, and a ready stream of finance to fuel that growth organically from your own profits or from investors.

Investor businesses

Entrepreneurial businesses and scalable growth businesses fall most easily into this area. They are characterised by external investors who contribute money, and often have a say in how the business is run. This can create conflict if the investors' views are at odds with the needs and dreams of the founders, owners or management.

It is not all about growth and money

No one business type is best, any can be a struggle or a great success. But you must be clear what you want at the outset. How should it serve you? And how will you know if it delivers that? You must make sure that your dreams and goals are aligned to the type of business you are running, giving you the best chance of a successful business alongside the life you want.

If stress and uncertainty filter through from work into the rest of your life, it can defeat the reasons you got into business in the first place. But there is a better way. The whole point of this book is to help you reduce or avoid many of the common mistakes, create simple plans and to keep you on a positive path. The better you do this, the better you align your business ambitions and your dreams, making running a business deeply rewarding.

Choose your direction and pace yourself

As this chapter is about your journey, I would like to say a few words about mindset, and the importance of matching your mindset and journey.

It is just like getting fit. You have to choose a fitness program which matches your ambition with the effort you wish to put in. You need to assess how fit you are now, how hard you are prepared to work, what results you want and by when. You have to build and develop your strength, flexibility and endurance over time. Lasting results rarely happen over-night. Success takes consistent action, in manageable steps, repeated frequently. You cannot get fit by going to the gym once, doing a massive workout, and then waiting to see the gains.

If you are ambitious, you have to consider your long term level of commitment. Growing a business is a marathon, not a sprint. You need to maintain your pace for the duration of the event, even if the challenges vary along the way. If you run a lifestyle business and you need to balance business commitments with the rest of your life, you need to assess how much time you have available, and work and plan accordingly.

Building a business is also like hiking up a mountain. You can only do it one step at a time. Experienced walkers reduce their pace when the going gets tough, but they keep going, their end goal firmly in mind. So pace yourself. Pause if you need to. Stop at key intervals. Look at the view. See how far you have come. Celebrate important markers in your progress. Above all, get back to the task and keep going. Remember, it is not what you do once in a while that matters, it is what you do consistently that makes the difference.

My Hopes for You

My belief is that we can all live better lives if we know how. I care deeply about the journey that we are on. I certainly want my own life to be as full, deep and rich as it can be, with a profound awareness of how it works at its best. I believe there are many of us who want the same. If you are read-ing this book, then I hope this includes you.

Modern physics teaches us that everything is connected, that every action has a related consequence, that everything we do, we essentially do to ourselves. In other words, we are all in this together. So, my hope is to offer you what I've always wanted for myself: to find the simplest means of understanding important subjects, giving us the power to make our lives better.

In my first career I was a designer. My passion was creating products. I designed all sorts of goods from toothbrushes, beer pumps, cosmetics packaging to computer casings and medical equipment. Although I designed them to the best of my ability, I never felt I was really making a big enough difference. As I looked at myself and the people around me, I realised that it wasn't the products in our hands but our mindset and psychology that mattered most.

It is how we think, feel and act
that makes the biggest difference
to our quality of life.

Thus began my slow transition from designing products to psychology, coaching and working with information. As we spend more time at work than in any other place, it became apparent that I could make a difference by improving the quality of work and the success people have in business, leading to the tools in this book.

My sincere hope is just as these tools have helped others before you, this book will help you be more successful in business, and in turn, help you and those you work with to live a better life.

What you have learned

- There are many reasons for being in business
- To identify your own reasons
- To match you ambitions and dreams to your business model
- To match your mindset to your end goal
- To pace yourself
  - Growing a business is a marathon not a sprint

Tips

- Consider your current situation
- Consider what has made you happiest in the past
- Consider what you believe will make you happiest in the future
- Keep business in perspective
  - It supports your life
  - Your business may fill your time, but it isn't life itself!

Required actions from this chapter

- Think about what you *really* want most
- Consider, do your business goals support the life you *really* wish to lead?
- Match your level of commitment to your desired end goal

In the next chapter

- Learn The Business Jet Engine® model

Section 2

Clearance for Take-Off
. . . get your plans in place

This is the diagnostic and planning section.

Here you will learn:

- The Business Jet Engine® model
- How to apply scores to your business at a basic and intermediate level
- A quick & simple method of business planning

For the year ahead you will be able to:

- Create a meaningful set of priorities for your own business
- Turn priorities into quarterly goals
- Turn quarterly goals into a one-month task list
- Learn top tips to keep you on track

CHAPTER THREE

The Business Jet Engine®
the story of your business?

The aim of this chapter is to

- Explain The Business Jet Engine® model
- Build it up in sequence
- Identify the areas and parts of your business
- Show how the areas and parts link together
- Relate this to your own business

Tips

If you have not already done this:

- Go to the free bonus content at www.businessjetengine.co.uk
- Watch the video animation
- Print out The Business Jet Engine® diagram in colour – you will need this!

Actions

- Think how The Business Jet Engine® applies to your own business

This is the story of how many businesses got started. This may not be exactly your story, but the story shows how the different parts of a business fit together and how this can be used as a diagnostic tool.

The Heart of The Business Jet Engine®

This is like the hard mechanics of our jet engine which is made up of three main parts:

- **The product:** the problem that your business solves for your customers and clients
- **Customer service:** how well you look after your clients during that process
- **Operations:** all the equipment, tools, processes that you need to deliver that product or service efficiently

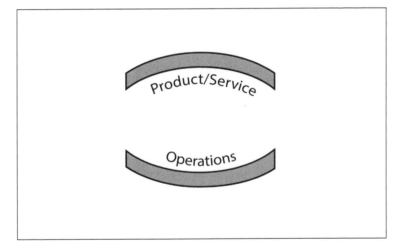

Your product

You are probably in business because you believe you have a good product or offering. You believe you know how to solve your clients' problems, and have a good way of doing so. If your business is based on a new idea, you have ideally tested it to know that it works, that there is sufficient demand, and people are willing to pay for it.

Customer service

You also hopefully know how to look after your clients whilst you deliver that product or service. If you have been in that industry a while, you should know what to do, and may have ideas about how to offer something better. If it is a new service, you will need to research what is expected or desired.

Operations

Again, if you are experienced in your industry, you should know what tools, equipment and processes you need to deliver your product or service. For a simple start-up business that might be simply a mobile phone, a business card, a website, equipment, and a place to work. With a more complex business, this could require investment, especially for businesses in manufacturing, logistics or regional retailing.

In addition, as a business founder you usually have some industry contacts, friends, relatives, or people you know who you have already spoken to about your new venture, who may have agreed to use you at the outset. Working with these existing contacts, your new business can be really busy for about six or nine months fulfilling those first orders. It looks like you made the right choice to start out on your own, and things couldn't be better. Then as the first flurry of orders get completed, you wake up one morning and realise something important:

> *'Help! My work is drying up! I have such a great idea,*
> *such a great product or service, I thought that by word*
> *of mouth my business would continue to fly.'*

And that is when you realise that there is more to business than just having a great product, service, and some slick operations. That is when you realise there is an important thing called sales and marketing. Which takes us on to exactly that . . .

Sales and Marketing

To make an engine work, you need an intake of air, in fact, vast quantities of it, which is no easy task. Sales and marketing is like having air coming into your engine. And to get your engine working, every business owner must master that process.

To help you think clearly, it is useful to differentiate between sales and marketing.

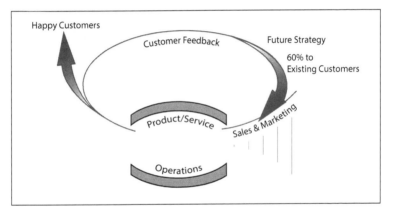

Sales

This is the part of the process when a potential customer makes an enquiry, and you then need to handle it effectively. This could be likened to fishing once you have a fish biting at the hook. Good salespeople are like good fisherman. You have to coax the fish to take the bait and then attempt to reel-in that fish.

Be too hasty, apply too much tension, too much pressure, the line might snap and the fish gets away. Equally if you are too lazy and lethargic, and don't strike, your fish will run off with your bait.

In sales, this is like failing to follow up enquiries, or not showing sufficient interest. Your customers will feel like they are unimportant to you and most likely go elsewhere.

Marketing

These are the activities that keep you in the forefront of a customer's mind, until they are ready to make an enquiry. It is all the activities that lure a fish to the hook. Good marketers realise that preceding an enquiry there is a journey that a potential customer needs to be coaxed along.

The customer sales journey

This is a series of stages where potential customers:

- Do not have, or think they have, the problem you can solve, yet
- Realise that they have the problem that you solve, though may not know about you
- Start to research how to solve that problem. A possible enquiry at this stage
- Create a shortlist of options to solve it.
- Make a decision, hopefully becoming your client

The customer sales journey recognises that most customers are not ready to buy right now. This is especially the case for major contracts which may take two to three years to come to fruition. Marketeers understand this and build a relationship over time. They tailor their messages to each part of their customer's journey, keeping themselves at the forefront of their mind until they are ready to make an enquiry or purchase.

Happy customers

Having got better at sales and marketing, your business now has air coming into the engine. You have a steady stream of clients to serve. The end result, the output you want, is happy customers.

Most business owners appreciate that without happy customers your business won't last long. Ideally, happy customers become raving fans and tell friends and contacts how good you are. They provide testimonials, giving new clients the reassurance they need to buy from you. They leave positive comments on review sites. And most importantly, they may come back to buy from you again.

Unhappy customers, at worst, want revenge. Everyone knows that bad news travels faster than good. You need happy customers to survive and thrive. If happy customers are essential, how do you know if you have them? Getting the answers to this leads us on to the next part of our story, and the next part of our Business Jet Engine®.

Customer feedback

How do you know what your clients truly value? This is one of the most important questions in business, yet the one least often asked.

Imagine this conversation:

> *'What do your customers really value from you most?'*
> *'Well, what we do of course.'*
> *'How do you know?'*
> *'Because they keep coming back and buying more from us.'*

But this is an assumption, not a fact, if you haven't *actually asked* the customer. As a business owner you need to know if your customers are returning because you offer the most reliable product, the highest quality, the most desirable brand, the cheapest price or because you offer easy parking, friendly banter or free coffee.

Asking the customer creates a feedback loop, where the answers lead to better product or service development and marketing, just as the expended air coming out of the jet engine has to be recycled by the atmosphere to one day be used again.

There are different levels of feedback:
- Listening for the good news
- Listening to both good *and* bad news
- Pro-actively asking for feedback
- Using independent research to ask for feedback

Independent research ensures even your most loyal customers, who would never want to upset you reveal what they wish you would improve.

Marketing to existing customers

Your business now has effective marketing and happy customers. This comes with a risk: focusing solely on growth. Winning new customers takes time and money. As a business becomes successful it can become obsessed with gaining new clients at the expense of looking after those they have. This can prove costly.

Some marketing gurus say that up to 60% of marketing activity should be back to your existing clients. They might want the same product or service again. They may like other products if offered. You need to keep existing customers fully aware of everything you offer. You may also want to send reminders for any reordering, and make requests for referrals.

Evolving a marketing-led future strategy

Finally, businesses may fail because they do not change or evolve. They keep offering the same old thing, not realising that their customers and market place have changed. What they produce is no longer wanted, or has become uncompetitive. Slowly sales dry up.

To avoid this, every year you need to choose one, two, or three key clients. Your ideal clients. The ones you want to build your future business around. Invite them out for an extended coffee, lunch or dinner and talk to them in a relaxed and informal manner. In this amiable environment, discuss where they are headed, now and in the future; what they want more of; what they can't get, from your business or elsewhere; what they are excited about; the things they are afraid of; the changes they foresee.

This gives you insight into where your core market is going and how to evolve with it.

With all this information, you can run an effective sales and marketing process. This results in a lot more air coming into the engine, which equates to more clients and customers coming through your door. Your engine seems to be turning nicely . . .

Finance

This is the point in our story where your product and service is good, your operations are running smoothly, and your sales and marketing cycle are keeping work coming in.

Your business now has an abundance of orders and you are working hard to fulfil them. You might even find yourself working flat-out for maybe one, two, or three years to capitalise on this influx of work. Things are looking great. You have never been busier.

As you gradually begin to get on top of it all, you decide to take time and review all the money you have made . . . and in exasperation, reality strikes, and you say,

'I'm working so hard, but where are my profits?
Why isn't there any money in the bank?'

This is a sobering moment lived by many business owners at this stage in their development. Just as they need quantities of air in their engine, they also need fuel. Where air is marketing, fuel is money, and the mixture has to be just right . . . you cannot run a business without taking finances seriously.

Pricing

Getting fuel to the engine starts with pricing. Getting the pricing right means that you can charge, with confidence, the absolute maximum possible and your clients still feel like they are getting great value

Being cheap is not the only way to offer great value. Even people who buy a top of the range Mercedes or Rolls-Royce, spending a comparatively large sum, want to feel like they have a good deal. They want to know, that compared to an equivalent purchase, they have value for money.

Even in a low-cost or budget marketplace, you still need to be charging as much as you can in that environment. You need to be charging as much as you can to achieve the next part of the engine.

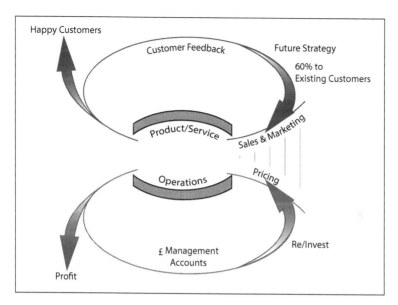

Profit

Focus on the fuel coming into the engine: correctly priced goods and services. Mixed with air, the sales and marketing activities, this creates your end goal, profit.

Profit can be likened to the exhaust gases coming out of the back of a jet. But why exhaust? In particular, some people think of profit as a dirty word. But we need to look beyond that. A business needs profit.

You need profit to retain in your business, maybe as a buffer for difficult times, or to pay dividends to shareholders or directors. You may need to pay off borrowings, or use it to re-invest and improve the business.

Without producing profit, there is no point in all the hard work of running your business. This is a classic mistake of both novice and experienced business owners. Profit does not just appear as a result of hard work. It appears as the result of intention and planning and the correct use of management accounts, which we will cover shortly.

Investing/re-investing

As you make a profit, exhaust gases can be used as they are in some of the most efficient engines: as a turbocharger. Profit can be recycled back into your business to re-invest in growth. In most businesses, retained profit gets offset by money re-invested. In other words, as one goes up, the other goes down. The more money you re-invest in your business, it stands to reason that there is less money in your bank account!

Management accounts

As you become serious about your finances, it becomes obvious why well-run businesses use regular management accounts as the most effective way to plan and track progress.

It helps to distinguish between management accounts and tax accounts. In simple terms tax accounts, often prepared by your accountant, are for working out your tax liability and what you need to pay the tax man.

Your management accounts are the information you need to plan and manage your business and include, at the least:

- a cash flow forecast, so you know when your cash is at risk and might run out
- a profit and loss statement, so each month you know if you are making money or losing money
- a balance sheet, which gives a snapshot of how much you own and how much you owe

To plan to make a profit, you also need a budget, ensuring revenues outweigh costs. With these your management accounts create measurements and controls, all in one place, to make sure that adequate financial progress is being made.

People

Your jet engine is roaring once you have mastered sales and marketing and finance. But there is a problem. The engine is roaring away bolted down in a garage or shed not going anywhere. Most people who build a business do so because they want to go somewhere. And for that you need more than an engine: you need wings. In The Business Jet Engine® model, people are the wings.

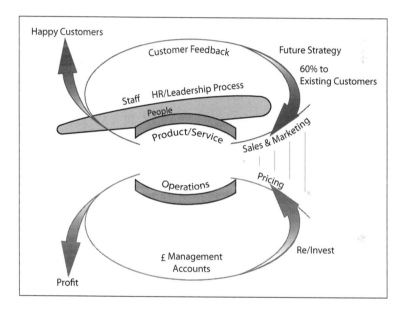

Quality of staff

When many businesses hire, they do so in a hurry. 'Quick, get some people in. Get bums on seats. We have work to do and can't wait. Anyone will do.' This often means they hire the best of three candidates from an inadequate shortlist, thinking this is the best they will find; resulting in a member of staff who isn't really suited to their role.

Having poor quality staff is like having an upside-down wing. As your plane goes along the runway, it is going to try and go down into the ground. If your business has average people, it is like having a flat profile wing and your plane will power along the runway using up fuel; all your time, money and energy, but never taking off.

When you have the correct profile people, A-Players, it is like having the correct profile wing. You get lift. Your business will take off and grow.

HR/leadership processes

To have fine control of your aircraft, you need fine control of your wings, which in business is your human resource, leadership and management processes. These may include:

- Hiring
- Job contracts/job descriptions
- Induction, training and career planning
- Leading, managing & motivating
- Reviews and appraisals
- Disciplinary procedures
- Exit procedures/letting people go

You need to hire, develop and lead top quality staff. Poor quality staff become 80% of your problems. Great staff become 80% of your solution. Great staff take problems away from you and bring them back solved, freeing up your time to plan, develop and grow your business.

Business Planning and KPIs

At last your business has taken off! Your engine, with its wings attached, is taking to the skies . . . But you had better think fast about where you are headed. Getting the engine working was only the beginning. Up in the air, forward planning is critical.

In a small business, planning might involve sitting in the cockpit, planning the route and checking all the instruments and controls. Flight paths need to be worked out, timings, navigation points etc. You need to ensure you have enough, fuel, water, food etc. on board to reach your destination safely.

With a bigger airline company, you may be at HQ considering the longer term future. Where will your passengers want to go, what will they pay, what must you charge, what are the available flight paths, what are current fuel prices and weather conditions? Or might you be affected by severe issues such as terrorism, war zones, natural disasters and so on.

Either way, as you think about planning, you need to learn some fundamentals.

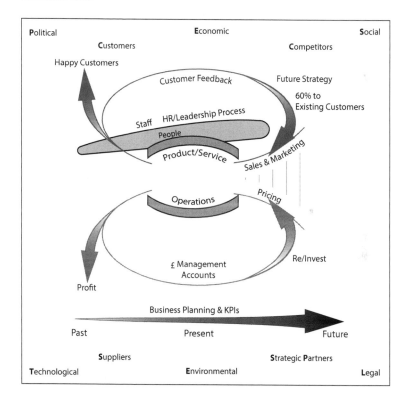

Competitive advantage

A key part of planning is having competitive advantage. You need a clear idea of what you offer your customers which is better or different to the competition – and not easily copied. Otherwise, why will customers buy from you when bombarded by choice?

The immediate market environment

You also need to continually check your immediate surroundings. In business this includes:

- Customers
- Competitors
- Suppliers
- Strategic partners

and with some businesses other special interest groups such as:

- Shareholders
- PR groups and the press
- Professional organisations & bodies

PESTEL

Beyond your immediate surroundings, there are six big game changers that can alter your industry or world overnight. They are made memorable by the acronym PESTEL:

- **P**olitical
- **E**conomic
- **S**ocial
- **T**echnological
- **E**nvironmental
- **L**egal

Depending on the size of your business and your resources, you may need to review potential opportunities and threats in these areas, maybe every six months or annually. If you do this, you reduce the risk of being caught out by dramatic changes.

Measuring and monitoring progress/KPIs

Alongside planning your flight, KPIs (Key Performance Indicators) are the indicators on the aircraft dashboard that tell you, the pilot, how you are progressing.

*You need to know that you are on course and that
everything in your aircraft is working as it should be.*

If not, you need to know in good time to take remedial action.

In business, alongside the planning activities, you need targets, measurements and controls that let you know that you are progressing as planned. These ideally include all the key parts of The Business Jet Engine®. At a minimum they include your basic financial tools; sales targets, a budget with income and expenditure, and the three cornerstones of management accounts: cash flow, profit & loss statement and a balance sheet.

This information needs to be produced at timely intervals. Some businesses with a large number of daily, unpredictable transactions may need this information daily, even hourly. For many businesses with a more predictable flow of sales, monthly or even quarterly figures, can provide adequate time for course correction if targets are not being met.

Summary of The Business Jet Engine®

We have now covered all the parts of The Business Jet Engine®.

The Heart of your Engine = Product, Service & Operations

The Product – The problem you solve for your clients

Customer Service – How well you look after your clients

Operations – How efficiently and effectively you deliver your product or service

This was followed by the need for air.

Air = Sales & Marketing

Sales – how effectively you convert enquiries

Marketing – how you keep at the forefront of people's minds, until they are ready to buy

Happy Customers – the essential end result for a sustainable business

Customer Feedback – how you know what your customers *truly* value

Marketing to Existing Clients – maximising hard won business

Future Strategy – evolving with your core client base

And the need for fuel to mix with air to fire your engine.

Fuel = Finance

Pricing – maximising what you charge against perceived client value

Profit – ensuring you make money for all your effort

Re-investment – turbo-charging growth

Management Accounts – ensuring you plan and measure to make a profit

With your engine firing, you need wings to make your business take off.

Wing = People

Staff – ensuring you have a high calibre team of A-players

HR & Leadership Processes – getting the best from your team or staff

With your airplane now in the air, you need to plan where you go and ensure you are on course.

Captain & Cockpit = Business Planning & KPIs

Inner Environment – customers, competitors, suppliers, strategic partners

Outer Environment – politics, economics, social, technology, environment, legal

All these parts need to be developed and working at their best. The engine needs to be smooth and powerful. The wing needs to give excellent lift. The pilot needs to plan ahead and keep the aircraft on course, at all times watching for changes in the aircraft, or environment, that could assist or bring their journey to a sudden end.

There is a lot to consider. Certainly so much more than just having a great product, service and some slick operations. For many, what started as a brave venture, has now become something far more. Running a business is about mastering a system of parts, requiring a host of new understanding and skills.

If you are up for the challenge, these parts can be learnt, in your own time as your business grows. The art is to prioritise. Prioritise what you need to learn. Prioritise what you change or improve, one step at a time. This book will show you how.

By learning these skills, you will become an ace pilot, with a deep understanding of your plane and the skies. When you master your craft, your business will really take off and fly!

What you have learned

- The Business Jet Engine® model
- How the model builds up in sequence
- The key areas and parts of your business
- How the areas and parts link together

Tips

If you have not already done this:
- Go to the free bonus content at www.businessjetengine.co.uk
- Watch the video animation
- Print out The Business Jet Engine® diagram in colour – you will need this!

Required actions from this chapter

- Think how The Business Jet Engine® applies to your own business

In the next chapter

- Apply scores to your business using the
  - Basic/fast scoring diagnostic questions
  - Intermediate diagnostic questions

CHAPTER FOUR

How is Your Business Jet Engine® Running?

scoring the diagnostic

The aim of this chapter is to

- Run a diagnostic on your own business
- Apply your scores to The Business Jet Engine® model, choosing your level
  - *Basic/Fast scoring*
  - *Intermediate*
- Evaluate your strengths and weaknesses

Tips

- Work on your own or with your team
  - For teams, see *Working with a team* in this chapter
- Remember, there are three levels of scoring throughout this book
  - Basic/Fast scoring
  - Intermediate
  - Advanced (in Section 3 Fine Tuning)

Actions

- Use a copy of The Business Jet Engine® diagram
  - Create a copy from this book

  or

  - Download a colour diagram from
    www.businessjetengine.co.uk
- Work through each part of The Business Jet Engine®
- Write your scores in coloured pen on your diagram
- Consider what prevents your score being a 10/10 in each area
- If working with your team, explore differences in scores

Applying Your Scores

In this section, you will take The Business Jet Engine® model and use it to help you understand where you are weak or strong in your own business and, in turn, establish your priorities for what to improve next. We will also look at an example business to see how The Business Jet Engine® model works. Make sure you have reviewed and downloaded the free tools at www.businessjetengine.co.uk before you move to this next stage.

To apply the model to your business, you want to score each key area out of 10, where:

 0 = Very weak/poor/no strength or ability

 5 = OK/adequate/just good enough

10 = Very strong/excellent/no room to improve

10/10 would mean that for your size of business that area could not be any better. It is simply as good as possible, with no room for improvement.

5/10 would mean that area works adequately. It just about meets your requirements to get by, but that is all.

0/10 means that area is totally neglected or couldn't be worse. You may not be aware of the importance of that area, and therefore no systems are in place. Or you have attempted to make it work but are unsuccessful.

Do not worry if you feel like you don't know everything about each area. Score yourself using your current knowledge to get started. What typically happens as your business grows and you get more experienced, is that your own depth of knowledge increases proportionally. Obviously a small simple business requires less knowledge than one which is much larger, so it is okay to start with your current level of awareness.

At the basic level, you may just be using your gut feeling, so trust the first scores that come to mind. At the intermediate levels you may be using facts and data to back up your opinions. Further on in the book, in the Fine Tuning section, you will be challenged in more detail, allowing you to stretch your awareness further.

For this first exercise, trust your gut feel and put down the first scores that come to mind, prompted by the simple questions in the overview exercise below. From my experience working with clients, this will give you a good enough snapshot of your strengths and weaknesses right now.

Considerations when Scoring

Speed and complexity of the analysis
First, you need to decide how involved you would like your analysis to be.

There are three levels of diagnostic questions:
- **Basic/fast scoring** – in this chapter
    - Fast and simple
    - Gives a quick insight into your major strengths and weaknesses
    - *Takes five minutes*
- **Intermediate** – in this chapter
    - More involved
    - Gives more detailed insight into strengths and weaknesses
    - Rapidly considers all parts of The Business Jet Engine®

- Relies on average scores for each area
- *Takes 15-30 minutes*
- **Advanced** – throughout each chapter of Section 3
  - Detailed and most time consuming – requires more effort and thought
  - Gives the most accurate analysis
  - Considers all parts of The Business Jet Engine® in greatest depth
  - Highlights the areas to develop next
  - *Takes one to two hours*

If you are new to business, do not feel pressured to absorb everything in this book immediately. Start with the basic level to give you a fast insight, then use this book frequently to strengthen your framework, one piece at a time.

If you are experienced in business, start with the intermediate scoring to gain an immediate insight, and to see the power of the model. When time permits, take yourself through the Fine Tuning section and advanced diagnostic questions to verify your results, and challenge yourself and your team.

Business timeframe

When scoring, consider how far ahead you wish to plan. There are two scenarios:

Against today

Score your business where it is right now, today. This option is for you if you have weaknesses you need to address immediately.

Against next year or your longterm plan

Score your business against a future timeframe, whether it be for the year ahead, or your next five to ten years. Score yourself against your future business model with the changes you require in place. By comparing where you are now against your longterm ideal, it will help you identify what is missing, so you put appropriate building blocks in place from today.

Working with a team

If you are working as a team, there are two main approaches.

Method 1: Work individually. Convene to compare scores

Each member of the team works through The Business Jet Engine® model on their own, in their own time. At an agreed time and date, the team convenes to compare scores. Work through each part of the model declaring scores and discussing differences as you go.

- When comparing, share what contributed to the score being, for example, 7/10
- Discuss what was missing that prevented the score being 10/10
- Look to establish a score that most of the team can agree upon

Method 2: Work through the model as a collective

Work through the model collectively, moving in order from one part to the next. Ensure each team member establishes a score in their head before anyone declares their view. When ready, share your thinking.

As with method one, discuss and compare differences. Seek to agree an average score for each part.

Basic/Fast Scoring Method

When to use it:

- If you are new to business or with limited experience

How to use it:

- You can do this exercise individually or with your team
- Trust your gut feelings
- Work quickly
- Be comparative against the other parts of the engine

This method uses a simplified version of The Business Jet Engine® and allows for crude average scores to be applied to the main parts of your business. As before, this method gives a quick snapshot of the condition of your business and should take no more than five to ten minutes.

Use the simple questions that follow and apply to the simplified diagram below.

The simplified Business Jet Engine® model

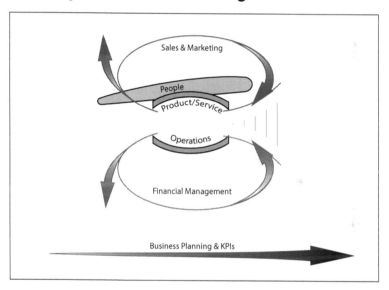

Score your business, from 0 to 10

Basic/Fast Scoring Diagnostic Questions

How well do you:

Product

Ensure your product or service solves your clients' problems?

Customer Service

Look after your clients whilst solving their problems?

Operations

Maximise all your operations that deliver that product
or service?

Sales & Marketing

Market yourself, handle sales and keep customers
informed of all your offers?

Finance

Manage finances, with sales targets, budgets and management
accounts focused on profit?

People

Recruit, train, develop and motivate the best people
in your industry?

Business Planning & KPIs

Plan for the short, medium and long term of your business?

Measure, monitor and review progress against
targets and KPIs?

Make alternative plans when required?

BizFit example – basic/fast scores

Here are the example results for BizFit, a fitness coaching business run by Sarah aimed at busy executives with little time to train. Sarah has completed the basic diagnostic questions. You can see how using even a simplified model highlights which parts of her business most need attention.

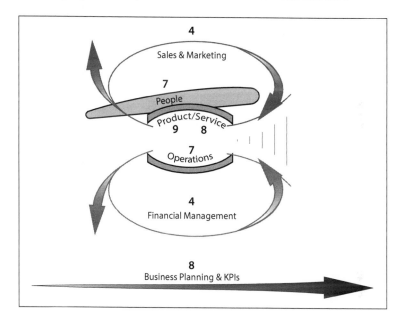

Her business has a great product and good customer service. Operations are relatively efficient, but sales and marketing activities leave room for improvement.

Sarah also has insufficient financial management. She is unclear on her budget and does not produce monthly management accounts. Sarah works hard, optimistic that her business will produce a profit.

Sarah's high score for planning, on reflection may be optimistic, and needs to be adjusted downwards. She based this on her clarity around her product/offering and how she wants it to develop. Clearly there are other parts of her business that she is ignoring and needs to plan more seriously.

Intermediate Scoring Method

When to use it:

- If you are experienced in business
- To quickly see your whole business as a system
- As a prelude to using the advanced method

How to use it:

- Individually or with your team
- Use the first answers in your head/your gut feeling
- Compare your answers, if working in a team or with others
- Reflect on what stops your scores being a 10/10. What is missing?
- Work moderately quickly for your first attempt
- Consider what facts or figures may validate your answers
- Build these, where possible, into future scorings
- Compare each part against the other parts of the engine

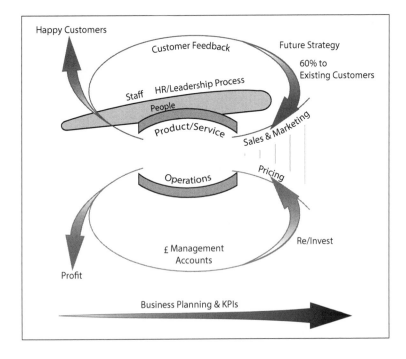

For this level you will use a more evolved diagram and consider the sub-sections of the major parts. For example, we previously only considered sales and marketing as one score, now we will score the subsections: sales, marketing, happy customers, customer feedback, marketing to existing customers and evolving your future strategy. We will do this for all the other areas as well.

Using the questions that follow, this exercise should take no more than 15 to 30 minutes to complete; an hour at the most if you debate each score with your team.

Remember:

  0 = Non-existent/shameful/woefully inadequate

  5 = Just adequate/passable/acceptable

10 = Exceptional/could not be better or improved

Intermediate Scoring Diagnostic Questions

How well do you:

The Heart of Your Engine

Product/Service

Solve your clients' problems?

Understand their ideal solution and what they value most?

Ensure your solutions come close to your clients' ideals?

Customer Service

Look after your clients whilst delivering that solution, so they feel loved and cared about?

Exceed your clients' expectations and create a Wow! factor or customer delight?

Look after your clients at *every* point of contact with you?

Operations

Ensure efficient and effective delivery of your product and service?

Identify your most costly systems and processes, and their associated risks?

Focus everyone on improving them for efficiency, cost effectiveness and risk reduction?

Sales & Marketing

Marketing

Stay at the forefront of customers' minds until they are ready to make an enquiry?

Follow a clear, evidence based marketing plan, and measure results?

Identify your market (who), message (what & why) and media channels (how)?

Sales

Handle sales enquiries, giving just the right level of attention?

Listen to and truly understand your clients' needs?

Ensure you have a sales pipeline matched to financial targets?

Happy Customers

Ensure you have delighted customers?

Ensure they will use you again?

Ensure they will recommend you to friends and contacts?

Customer Feedback

Collect customer feedback and then act on that information?[1]

Obtain feedback from all your customers?

Obtain highly specific feedback from your most valuable customers?

Marketing to Existing Customers

Focus 60% of your marketing to existing customers?

Ensure they are aware of all you offer?

Comprehensively ask them to recommend you or make referrals?

Evolving Future Strategy

Identify your future ideal customers?

Have in-depth, relaxed conversations, annually, with one to three of your ideal clients?

Use these key insights to evolve your business for the future?

Finance

Pricing

Charge as much as your market will stand, whilst your clients
still get great value from you?

Research this with your clients and competitors?

Test higher pricing in your market?

Profit

Retain profit in your business, i.e. three to six months' reserves
in the bank?

Pay appropriate dividends to directors, shareholders
and investors?

Pay-off any debt?

Investment/Re-Investment

Ensure your resources are up to date with:[2]

People and training?

Equipment and technology?

Systems and processes for each part of your
Business Jet Engine®?

Management Accounts

Produce timely management accounts with sufficient
information to drive your business?[3]

Produce sales targets, budgets, cash flow, profit & loss and
balance sheet statements?

Assess your financial performance and needs, now
and in the future?

People

Staff

Retain the best staff in your industry?[4]

Measure your staff compared to other, especially comparable, industries?

Review the quality of your staff and identify who needs particular support?

HR & Leadership Processes

Ensure you hire, train, develop, engage, appraise, motivate and retain the best possible staff, aligned with the company vision and goals?

Follow HR (Human Resource) best practice?

Consciously develop leadership excellence at all levels of your business?

Business Planning & KPIs

Business Planning

Ensure time to work *on* your business, not just *in* it?

Create short, medium and long term plans for your business?

Consider all your internal & external factors:

Internal: customers, competitors, suppliers, strategic partners etc.?

External: political, economic, social, technological, environmental, legal?

Measuring & Monitoring/KPIs

Measure and monitor progress using KPIs in all key areas?

Take remedial action as required?

[1] Suggested scoring for this area:

    Open to hearing good news = 0–3

    Open to hearing good and bad news = 4–5

    Pro-actively seek feedback = 6–7

    Get independent feedback through an external resource = 8–10

[2] Suggested scoring for these areas:

    Falling behind = 4 or below

    Just keeping up = around 5

    Adequately up-to-date = 6–7

    Fully up-to-date = 8–10

[3] Suggested scoring for this area:

    Only produce annual tax accounts = 0–3

    Bookkeeping up-to-date, but no timely reporting = 4–5

    Produce timely reports with sufficient information for analysis = 6–7

    Produce timely reports with comprehensive information for analysis and planning, plus follow-up actions = 8–10

[4] Suggested scoring for this area:

    D-Players. Below average. Cost more than they earn = 3–5

    C-Players. Average. Loyal foot-soldiers = 5–7

    B-Players. Almost the best, but ambitious = 7–8

    A-Players. The very best in your industry = 8–10

REMINDER: Key action – do this now!

- Download your Business Jet Engine® colour diagram from the free tools at www.businessjetengine.co.uk
- Use the questions above to enter scores for your business
- Calculate an average score for each part

- Write your scores on your Business Jet Engine® diagram
  - Ideally using a coloured/red pen
- **Make sure you have done this before moving on to Chapter 5**

Remember

- Should you wish to diagnose your business in greater depth there is an advanced scoring method in Section 3

BizFit example – *intermediate scoring method*

Here are BizFit's revised scores, with the intermediate diagnostic questions applied.

You can see how intermediate scoring gives greater insight into Sarah's business. It shows how each part of her business is inter-connected, how a weakness in one area may lead to a weakness in another part of the system. With this more detailed scoring, as you learn how to read the diagnostic, the Business Jet Engine® model comes alive.

In addition, this process forces you to consider what may be missing in each part of your own business. To arrive at a meaningful score, you must also ask yourself, 'What is missing that prevents this score being a ten?' I sometimes call these missing factors *The Missing X*. This question, 'What's the missing X?' is almost more important than your actual score.

The real value is in what you next need to improve
which is hiding in the missing X!

Explaining the scores

This fitness coaching business, aimed at busy executives with little time to train, is run by Sarah the owner and principal trainer. She also employs two part-time trainers and an admin assistant.

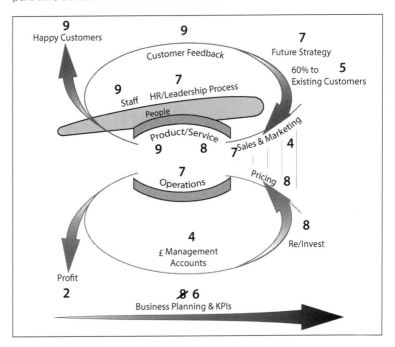

The Heart of the Engine
Product = 9/10

Sarah has a lot of confidence in their product. They are good at helping their clients make the changes they want and have a high success rate. They measure and monitor those changes with their clients, giving them confidence in this score. Sarah and her coaches do their best to stay up to date with developments in their field and are often ahead of the competition.

Missing 1 = there is always something new to learn, test and evaluate, preventing their score ever being a 10.

Customer service = 8/10

Sarah believes they give good customer service, working passionately when face-to-face ensuring clients feel cared about from first contact. The team often give more than clients pay for.

Missing 2 = more contact is needed between sessions, especially if clients are struggling when training on their own.

Operations = 7/10

Most of their day-to-day office systems are relatively efficient. They are organised with their client work and have routine ways of doing things. They use templates and checklists for many repeat activities, especially preparing for client sessions and preparing exercise equipment.

Missing 3 = less urgent paperwork builds up. Non-client to-do items can get forgotten which could be scheduled into the online diary with alerts and reminders.

Improvements could include: using CRM software to schedule more frequent client contact, and linked to their sales and marketing, which can be ad hoc; online accounts software to streamline their book-keeping, invoicing and VAT.

Sales & Marketing
Sales = 7/10

They know how many clients they need each year to achieve their desired sales revenue. When they have a clearly genuine enquiry they are good at converting that into a new client. The team ensure they understand their client's needs, explain how they can help and offer a free taster session.

Missing 3 = casual enquiries, especially when the team are busy, can get overlooked. They could possibly gain an extra 10% of sales by better use of a CRM (customer relationship management system) to record all enquiries and schedule a specific member of the team to follow-up.

They also do not use a sales pipeline to predict new and returning clients throughout the year, which would give them greater focus on the sales necessary to hit their sales targets.

Marketing = 4/10
Sarah and the team are clear on their brand and competitive advantage. They have a good reputation, network locally, use social media and exhibit at business exhibitions.

> **Missing 6** = all their activities are ad hoc. They do not work to a budget or a plan. They need to develop a marketing budget and be able to measure the success of their marketing activities to improve their return on investment.

Happy customers = 9/10
Clients offer high praise for the service they receive and are rarely able to suggest improvements when asked.

> **Missing 1** = a more personalised approach for certain clients who may require, for example, additional support between sessions or a customised way of working.

Customer feedback = 9/10
The team check that clients are happy at the end of every session. In addition, Sarah uses an independent marketing agency to call all her clients, at least once annually. This provides excellent feedback which can be turned into approved testimonials.

> **Missing 1** = clients are in an electronic address book, not on a CRM, so follow-up calls can get missed.

Marketing to existing clients = 5/10
As the team work face-to-face with their clients, they are in a good position to offer additional products and services. However, whilst in session,

the team are focused on training not sales, and may not think to discuss additional training options with their clients, even if those options may prove to be of interest.

Missing 5 = not consistently highlighting additional products and services, face-to-face, via emails and social media as part of the marketing plan. Not implementing a proven referral program.

Evolving future strategy = 7/10

Sarah's team work closely with their clients at a personal level. This allows the team to stay closely attuned to their clients' needs, now and in the future.

Missing 3 = more in-depth conversations away from the training sessions about wider issues and how their clients' needs may change in the future.

Finance
Pricing = 8/10

Sarah is aware of her pricing compared to similar businesses in her area and having increased her prices progressively year-on-year is intentionally at the upper end of her market. She also has a range of training options to appeal to different price points.

Missing 2 = Sarah doesn't have total confidence that she truly understands what her clients would pay for a top-level service. She knows she is near the top of the market, but could she charge more? Is there a VIP package she has not considered?

Profit = 2/10

The business has invested heavily in the last two years, taking on new premises, staff, furniture and equipment. They are able to pay the monthly instalments towards their loan, and pay staff and suppliers. Sarah takes a small dividend. However there is little spare cash in the bank to ease cash flow or to create a long-term buffer.

Missing 8 = an accurately defined budget to ensure profit against expenses, pay off the loan and create a monthly standing order to create a cash reserve in the savings account.

The need to increase sales revenue for more generous profits may also motivate them to create a proper sales pipeline.

Investments = 8/10

Having recently invested in the business, it is well resourced with staff, furniture, equipment, IT and some updated software. However, this has had an impact on profits.

Missing 2 = CRM and online bookkeeping software.

Management accounts = 4/10

Sarah has clear sales targets for the year, and knows exactly what the team needs to achieve. With the help of her admin assistant, she is always up-to-date with her bookkeeping. Everything is reconciled at least weekly or fortnightly, and they have accurate cash flow projections. Corporation tax and VAT are estimated at the start of each year, with a corresponding monthly standing order into their savings account. This ensures money is put aside for when these payments are due.

Missing 6 = a more accurate budget so they spend to agreed amounts, especially marketing. Monthly reporting of profit & loss against budget, and a balance sheet report. Consideration of any other financial KPIs, such as cost of sales. Creating plans to improve financial performance.

People
Staff = 9/10

Sarah is confident she has talented, motivated staff who get on well with clients and work well as a team.

Missing 1 = maybe additional training or a team away-day?

Human resources and leadership processes = 7/10

Sarah takes pride in how carefully she selects her team and only hires a new member when she is confident that they meet her highest standards. All HR paperwork is adequately in place, including job contracts and a staff handbook. Everyone is motivated and focused on the company goals.

Missing 3 = closer management of secondary tasks with scheduled briefings and follow-up meetings to discuss progress. Identify and implement any training if required.

Business planning and KPIs
Business planning = 8/10

Sarah and the team are clear on their brand and what gives them competitive advantage. They know what makes them successful and where they are headed in the short and long term.

Missing 2 = as already discussed in other areas: financial budget, monthly financial reporting, marketing budget and agreed measurements to improve ROI and a sales pipeline. Annual team away-day to consider long-term challenges and opportunities?

KPIs = 4/10

They work to only a few KPIs, but this is not comprehensive.

Missing 6 = time to identify key business drivers and produce a comprehensive set of KPIs.

On reflection, by averaging her planning and KPIs score, Sarah decided to downgrade her overall business planning score from an 8 to a 6.

Advanced Scoring Method

This method is the most detailed. If you want to proceed to this level, review Section 3: Fine Tuning. Here you will find basic concepts and a comprehensive set of diagnostic questions applied to each part of your

Business Jet Engine®. Where you excel, you should be more expert than the concepts in this book. Where you are weak, it should reveal what you most neglect and test the limits of your knowledge.

What you have learned

- Running a diagnostic on your jet engine helps you to:
  - See your business as a whole
  - See where you place too much focus – typically your strengths
  - See what you neglect – typically your weaknesses
  - Consider what you don't yet know
  - Think about what you *could* be doing
- If you've completed this exercise with your team, you should have:
  - A shared team understanding of the condition of your engine

Tips

- Work on your own or with your team
  - For teams, see *Working with a team* in this chapter
- Remember, there are three levels of scoring throughout this book
  - Basic/Fast scoring
  - Intermediate
  - Advanced

Required actions from this chapter

- Use a copy of The Business Jet Engine® diagram
  - Create a copy from this book

  or

  - Download a colour diagram from www.businessjetengine.co.uk
- Work through each part of The Business Jet Engine®
- Write your scores in coloured pen on your diagram
- Consider what prevents your score being a 10/10 in each area
- If working with your team, explore differences in scores

In the next chapter

- Turn your scores into your priority areas to improve

CHAPTER FIVE

Creating Groups
your engine as a system

The aim of this chapter is to

- See your business as a system
- Understand the real blocks to running it smoothly
- Identify your three priority areas to improve this year
- Be ready to develop your annual priorities and plans in
  Chapter 6

Tips

- Look for what will create the greatest impact in your business
- Be realistic with what you can achieve in a year
- Try variations of groupings and see which looks most effective
  - Use a coloured/orange pen for contrast
- Trust that the process becomes easier with experience

Actions

- Use copies of your Business Jet Engine® diagram with your
  scores applied
- Identify root causes first

> - Create groupings based on those root causes
> - Create multiple options using copies
> - Compare your options. What would have greatest longterm impact?
> - Decide on your final three priority areas to fix this year

In this section, you will take your Business Jet Engine®, the scores you have applied to it, and establish some logical groupings by circling key areas on your diagram. These circled groupings form the priority areas that you wish to improve and will have the greatest impact on your business in the next 12 months.

This exercise also helps you see your business visually laid out as a system, aiding your ability to see root causes and knock-on effects.

It forces you to think how poor performance in one area
may lead to a poor performance in another.

To help you with this process, we will use examples to illustrate some of the most common links which may be present in your business.

Here are two common root causes and the problems they lead to:
Poor HR and leadership processes:
  - leads to hiring mediocre staff who create underperformance in other parts of the business, especially operations and customer service.

Poor financial planning and a lack of management accounts:
  - leads to a lack of profit and an inability to re-invest, even if accompanied by strong pricing and sales.

This process becomes easier with practice and experience: this is more true of this stage than any other. Over time, you will find it easier to identify your core issues as you become more attuned to cause and effect relationships. And as you develop plans which you put into action, you will become more realistic as to what your business can improve and achieve in a year.

Three Concepts that will Help You

In Chapter 6. Planning Your Flight Path, we will discuss three concepts that will help you with your analysis and planning:

- The 80/20 rule
- The power of threes
- Strategic goals *vs* day-to-day goals

As they are also useful for our next task, here's a brief introduction.

The 80/20 rule

The 80/20 rule suggests that 20% of what you do produces 80% of the results that you want. The proportions may not always be exactly this. It may be 70/30, 60/40, 90/10. The key to using the 80/20 rule is to keep focusing on the smallest part, that if improved, will have the greatest overall benefit.

The power of threes

When you create too many goals or projects, people struggle to remember them all. When you restrict this number to three, most people find them more memorable.

Strategic goals vs day-to-day goals

Day-to-day goals can be described as the tasks you are already doing to make your business work, which you can improve incrementally. Strategic goals, however, require a more significant change: a systemic change to how you currently do things, and require more time and effort.

Marking the Groupings

Make multiple copies of your Business Jet Engine® so you can compare the options you create. Use a coloured pen for contrast (I like orange for this task) to circle the lowest scores most ripe for improvement, and then your groupings.

Circles

Start by identifying the three lowest scores that appear to be your most important root causes. Use a solid circle so it stands out.

Dashed lines

Use a dashed line to:

- Create your priority areas. Typically try and identify no more than three
- Circle other low scores you would like to address if you have additional resources
- Circle root causes of secondary importance that you wish to bear in mind

Common Groupings – examples

These are taken from:

- Three micro-businesses
- Two medium size businesses
- Sarah's FitBiz example

They are presented with background information explaining why they are grouped as they are. Some of these cause and effect relationships may be present in your business.

Micro-Biz 1

This set of scores is typical for many small businesses. The leader is busy working in the business, with insufficient time to manage or plan. Their marketing is ad-hoc and in-house.

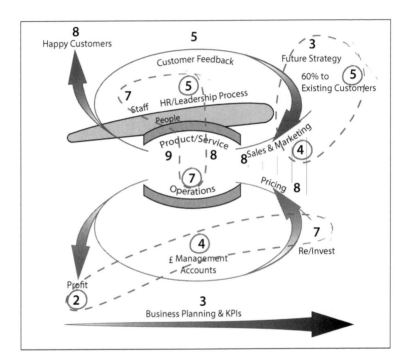

Company background:
- Established 5+ years
- 5–7 staff
- Turnover of circa £350k

Key issue:
- MD busy working in the business

Leads to:
- Insufficient time for good HR and leadership processes
- Mostly good staff, some mediocre to poor staff
- Some operational systems not established
- Where they exist, operational systems not always followed

Key issue:

- Average bookkeeping
- No regular management accounts
- Lack of financial plans for profit

Leads to:

- Low profit
- Unable to maximise re-investment

Key issue:

- Insufficient marketing plans and activity
- Insufficient marketing to existing clients

Leads to:

- Only an average volume of sales through the business
- Original growth slowed
- Reached a plateau?

Micro-Biz 2

This business is newer and has fewer resources than Example 1, leading to stalled growth. The priority areas are similar, but tightly focused to keep plans realistic.

Company background:

- Established 3–5 years
- 4–5 staff
- Turnover of circa £200–250k

Key issue:

- MD not managing and developing staff

Leads to:

- MD overworked delivering to high standards
- Staff not working to full potential
- MD burn-out
- Other areas of the business under-developed

Key issue:

- Just keeping on-top of the bookkeeping
- No financial plans and targets

Leads to:

- Low profit & slow growth

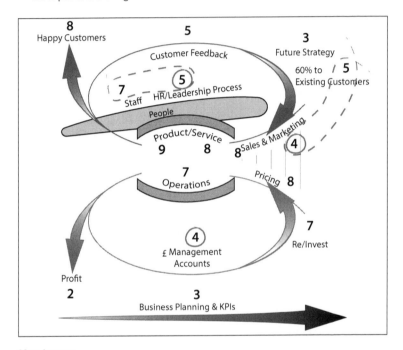

Key issue:

- MD driving most activities
- No time or desire to attract additional work

Leads to:

- Slow growth

Micro-Biz 3

This business by contrast with the previous examples is highly proficient at sales and marketing. The MD works long hours, has excellent staff and processes in place. Time is scarce to develop better financial or business plans, resulting in them being overworked for little reward.

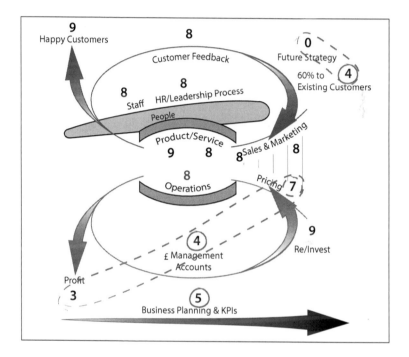

Company background:

- Established 5+ years
- 5 staff
- Turnover of circa £250k
- Recent family loan for investment in office upgrade

Key issue:

- No financial plans for profit

Leads to:

- Undercharging for excellent work
- Very busy
- Low profit
- Financial uncertainty

Key issue:

- No time for business planning

Leads to:

- Massive uncertainty
- Really busy, but where is it all going?

Key issue:

- Insufficient time spent marketing to existing clients

Leads to:

- Extra time required to attract new clients
- No time for better planning or delegating to staff

Medio-Biz 1

Here is an example medium sized company. It is well established, but sales are in decline.

Company background:

- Established 15+ years
- 30 staff
- Turnover £4M+
- Full time finance manager
- HR outsourced

Key issue:

- Established departments busy working independently
- Senior managers (SMT) not working as a team
- No-one driving a management process

Leads to:

- Staff busy doing what they have always done
- No agreed business plan
- Risk of losing competitive advantage
- Risk of losing market share

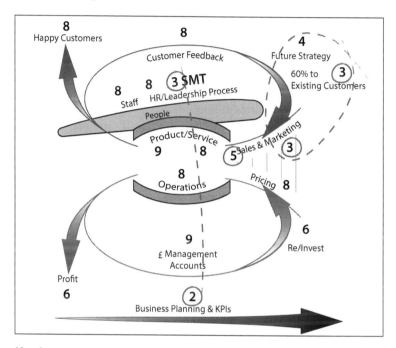

Key issue:

- Business built on outdated relationships
- No one responsible for marketing

Leads to:

- No clear marketing message or position
- An ever-decreasing pool of leads

Key issue:

- Ad-hoc sales activities

Leads to:

- No sales pipeline or measurable activity
- Staff not held to account or motivated to deliver new leads

Medio-Biz 2

Here is an example medium business. It is well established, has over fifty staff. Turnover exceeds £10M, but with size comes the challenge of retaining standards and quality.

Company background:

- Established 20+ years
- 50+ staff
- Turnover £10M+
- Managers in place for all departments

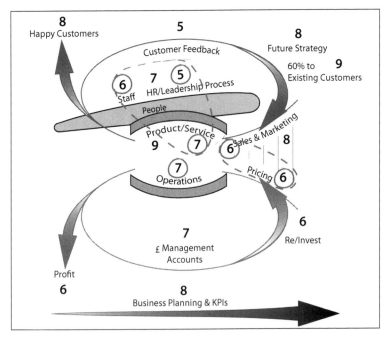

Key issue:

- All managers working at capacity doing 'their job'
- Focus on delivery, not people
- Under-developed culture of leadership and management

Leads to:

- No time to hire carefully
- Too many underperforming staff
- Top performers missing in key roles
- Decline in customer service

Key issue:

- Lack of communication between sales and quotation department

Leads to:

- Inconsistent pricing
- Underpriced goods and lost profit

Key issue:

- Under-developed systems and processes

Leads to:

- Inconsistent ways of doing some key tasks
- Frustrations between staff
- Difficulty delivering all projects on time, within budget at the right quality

FitBiz – *explaining the groupings*

Let us return to Sarah and her fitness business from Chapter 4.

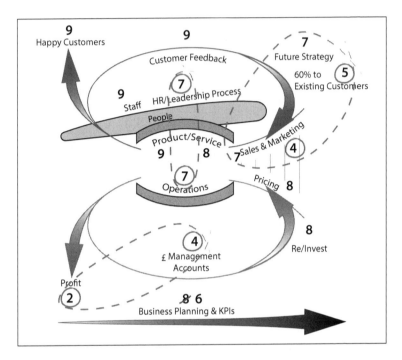

Company background:

- Established 5+ years
- 1 full-time, 3 part-time staff
- Turnover £135k

Leadership and operations
Operations

Their systems for working with clients are relatively efficient. They use set routines, checklists and templates for this core work. However, less urgent paperwork builds up and they know they could have better processes for client contact between sessions, and sales and marketing activities.

Leadership

Sarah has great staff who are motivated to make the business work. However, Sarah puts too much on herself. If she identified key tasks to delegate and manage through others, the business could be more efficient. This may also free her to implement a desired online accounts package and CRM (customer relationship management) system.

Key issue:
- Sarah keeps too many tasks to herself which she could delegate

Leads to:
- No time for better planning
- No time to research and implement a CRM system
- No time to research and implement an online accounting package
- All would aid greater operational efficiency

Sales and marketing

The team are good at converting 'hot' leads, but casual enquiries can go cold, especially when they are busy. They have a good reputation and network locally, use social media and exhibit at business exhibitions. However, anything beyond that is ad-hoc and they have no marketing plan.

They have a good client retention rate, but rarely discuss other programmes or options that may appeal. The team develop close relationships with their clients, but rarely have in-depth conversations away from training about their clients' long-term needs.

Key issue:
- Marketing is ad-hoc
- No CRM

Leads to:
- Lack of consistent marketing
- Lost warm leads
- Do not maximise the value they can offer existing clients

Financial performance

Sarah has clear sales targets, is always up-to-date with her bookkeeping, has accurate cash flow projections and puts money aside each month for corporation tax and VAT. However, she has not had time to create a budget or create monthly management accounts. And having made some big investments, there is little profit in the bank to create a cash buffer.

Key issue:

- Sarah is too busy to:
    - create a budget
    - produce management accounts, especially a monthly profit & loss statement
    - improve financial performance

Leads to:

- Uncertainty around expenses. What can they spend on marketing, software etc?
- Vulnerable cashflow. It is often 'a bit tight'
- Lack of profit

FitBiz summary

You can see that in Sarah's business these three priority areas interlink. A deficiency in one area leads to a deficiency in another. Because Sarah does not delegate enough, she is short on time, therefore improvements in key operations get postponed.

Inefficient operations take up staff time, with everyone working to capacity but missing other important tasks. Lack of time also leads to inefficient or neglected marketing, which leads to a loss of potential sales.

Without time to create a budget, there is no certainty around profit, leaving Sarah reluctant to invest in software. Their marketing and financial systems remain inefficient, everyone remains at capacity and the cycle continues.

Identifying Key Areas to Improve for Your Own Business

Having looked at these examples, you need to consider your own priority areas and groupings. Remember to apply the 80/20 rule to find the improvements that have greatest net effect. Remember the power of threes and try limiting yourself to three areas to improve. The bigger your resources, the more ambitious you can be.

> *Focus on the strategic changes that put your business up a gear, not just slightly faster in the same gear.*

Look at your business as a system of connected parts. Look for related groups of scores that sit nicely together, creating your priority areas. If you have made copies of your diagram with your scores applied, try various combinations of groupings. Decide which option looks most appropriate for you and your business.

As with all stages of The Business Jet Engine®, this process becomes easier with repetition. Root causes become more apparent. Interconnections easier to spot. Which areas to improve and in which order become second nature. As with all things, practice makes perfect.

Allow yourself an acceptable amount of time at this stage, and refrain from exceeding it. Towards the end of your allocated time decide which option will have the greatest long-term effect. If you are unsure, make a decision anyway. Then go for it. You will make more progress than taking no action. You will almost certainly be heading in a better direction than doing nothing through indecision.

What you have learned

- With all these examples, considering the priority areas forces you to think about:
  - Your business as a system
  - How weakness in one area leads to weakness in another
  - What needs to be improved? What is missing that stops it being perfect?
  - What resources do you have to improve these areas?
  - What you can achieve in a year

Tips

- Look for what will create the greatest impact in your business
- Be realistic with what you can achieve in a year
- Try variations of groupings and see which looks most effective
  - Use a coloured/orange pen for contrast
- Trust that the process becomes easier with experience

Required actions from this chapter

- Use The Business Jet Engine® diagram with your scores applied
- Make multiple copies so you can compare options
- Circle your three weakest root causes. Use solid lines
  - Consider why they underperform and what that leads to
- Create groupings based on those root causes. Use dashed lines
- Create multiple options using copies
- Compare your options. What would have greatest longterm impact?
- Decide on your final three priority areas to fix this year

In the next chapter

- Turn your priority areas into plans

Planning Your Flight Path
making a plan that will work

The aim of this chapter is to

- Help you avoid a major planning mistake
- Explain three key concepts
- Show you how to turn your priority areas into simple plans

Tips

- Be prepared to create several drafts
- Refer to your work in the previous two chapters
- It is better to write something than nothing
- You can revisit your plans – improve them in stages
- If new to planning, remember, your plans will become better with practice

Actions

- Use your Business Jet Engine® diagram with your marked priority areas
- Develop your thinking into written plans by writing:
  - Three annual priorities

> – Three subgoals for each priority
> – A plan for your first quarter
> – A task-list for your first month

Having diagnosed your business and created your priority groups to improve, you need to turn your thinking into actions.

To ensure your planning is a success, it is important to consider why so many businesses fail. The UK Government Office for National Statistics reports that the five-year survival rate for businesses that launched in 2009 and remained active in 2014 was 41.7%. Meaning:

Almost 60% of start-ups fail within five years.

From experience, most businesses struggle due to one of the following:

- Insufficient cash
- An inadequately thought through business model
- A lack of competitive advantage
- Poor planning
- Trying to change too many things at once
- Changing nothing due to uncertainty and overwhelm

The last three relate to unclear thinking and a lack of practical plans. To address this issue, this chapter will show you how to create *simple* plans. If you are a time-stretched business owner, these are of great value by being:

- Focused only on what is important
- Focused only on what is achievable
- Quick to create
- Quick to review
- Quick to update

Concepts for Planning

Three concepts which will help you turn your groupings into usable plans are:

- The 80/20 rule
- The power of threes
- Strategic goals *vs* day-to-day goals

Be aware that a major mistake when planning is getting bogged down in the details too soon. If you try to include every factor which may appear relevant, it:

- Slows the process
- Introduces too much uncertainty
- Obscures the big picture

You need to see the big picture first, using approximate figures and estimates, to reassure yourself that you are heading in the right direction. Clearly, if you are heading in the wrong direction, adding infinite detail is a waste of time.

Once you are confident of your direction, you can increase the accuracy of your figures, evolving from annual priorities, into quarterly plans, then manageable monthly tasks.

The 80/20 rule

The 80/20 rule, also known as The Pareto Principle or 'the law of the vital few and the trivial many', is highly valuable. It can be applied to every aspect of your personal and business activities. The key principle being that:

- There is an inequality in the results of our efforts
- We need to focus on what is most fruitful

The Italian economist Vilfredo Pareto (1848-1923) studied patterns of wealth in Europe. He discovered a reasonably consistent ratio: 80% of the land or wealth was owned by 20% of the population. This principle was developed further in the 1930-40s by the quality management pioneer, Dr. Joseph Juran. He recognised that the principle of disproportion could be applied in many other realms.

The 80/20 rule suggests that 20% of what we do produces 80% of the results that we want. The proportions may not always be exactly this; it may be 70/30, 60/40, 90/10. The exact ratio is not important.

The key point is there is a disproportion of effort to achieve a result.

So the key to using the 80/20 rule is to:

Identify the 20% to improve that will affect 80% of your results.

For example, if you need to improve your sales revenue, you might approach this as many business owners do, and raise your sales and marketing activity across your whole product range. By contrast, you could be much smarter in your approach. You could identify your most profitable product and the target audience most receptive to buying it. This one product may represent only 20% of your product range, and be relevant to only 20% of your total market. Then focus all your additional resources on marketing that one product to that market. From this precise targeting, you would normally see a greater increase in your sales and profits than if you increased your marketing across the board.

The key questions raised by the 80/20 principle are:
* What is most effective in producing the results you want?
* Can you increase this or do it more?
* What is least effective in producing the results you want?
* Can you decrease that or do it less?

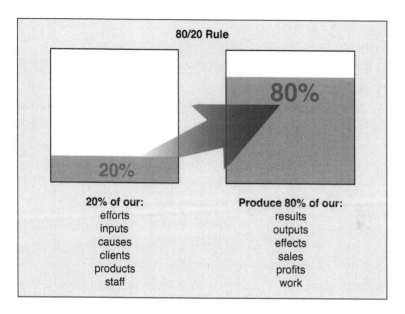

The power of threes

When you create your annual priorities, ideally limit them to three (not including your sub-goals). If you have less than three priorities, insufficient progress is made. More than three, and it becomes hard to focus. In addition, you want to engage your staff in your plans, and most people do not easily remember more than three things.

When everyone has your priorities in mind, these act as a focus against which all decisions are made. When you have five, seven, or more priorities, then it becomes easy to forget what is important and get side-tracked along the way.

Strategic goals vs day-to-day goals

Do you know the difference between a strategic goal and day-to-day goal?

- Day-to-day goals are what you normally do to make your business work
- Strategic goals fundamentally improve your long-term prospects

With your day-to-day goals, the backbone of your current business, you should always be looking to make small incremental improvements. This is like accelerating in a car whilst staying in the same gear. You gradually speed up, but there is a limit to how fast you can go in that gear.

Strategic goals require a more significant change. These are where you aim to make a significant difference a year or so from now. This is like changing up a gear in order to go much faster but in an old-fashioned car, at a time when changing gear was a risky business. It involved double de-clutching, a heavy gear-change action, the risk of missing it and a potential loss of momentum. The danger was that the engine would not be able to pick up from lower revs in the higher gear, and you would have to change back down, regain momentum and try again.

This is much like the challenges of growth in your business where significant change requires significant action and will rarely be reached by gradual improvement. It requires a total change in how you currently do things, like moving to a brand new computer system, a new office, or introducing a new manufacturing process. If you are already near capacity, systemic change requires time, money and energy that is hard for you to find. You need to carve out time from your day-to-day activities. You need to dig deep and find additional reserves to take action, and think in new and creative ways.

The key here is to ask:
- What are the areas where I am weakest and really need to improve?
- What are the areas where I could grasp the greatest opportunities?

Creating Annual Priorities, Quarterly Plans and Monthly Tasks

In the previous sections, you have diagnosed the strengths and weaknesses of your business and identified your priority areas to move you ahead. This should give you:
- **What** you need to improve
- **Why** this will help you long-term

You now need to convert that work into plans:
- **How** you will turn it into actions

If you are experienced, you may know exactly what you need to do next. If you are less experienced, and therefore uncertain, you may hesitate or start to panic. To help with this, aim to find a balance between making progress now based on your current knowledge and building precise plans in the future.

If you feel uncertain what to do next

Return to the diagnostic questions at whichever level you chose to work. Review the areas that you gave the lowest scores. The actual scores you gave are in many ways irrelevant. The real value is in what you believe to be missing that prevented that score from being 10/10.

1) Ensure you have really considered for each low score what is missing that prevents it from being a 10 based on your current knowledge.

Write down your answers to:
- What is not working well?
- Who is struggling to deliver in that area?
- What do you think is missing?
- What do you or your team not know enough about?
- Using your best guess, what needs to change or improve?
- What could you put in place to fix this?
- In what area do you need to do research, or get support or training?

2) If you are still stuck, read the summaries in Section 3, Fine Tuning for the basic concepts that will help you. If your knowledge exceeds the summaries, test yourself against the advanced diagnostic questions in those areas.

3) If you are still stuck, consider if you could:
- Talk to an experienced business owner?
  - They may have ideas to offer about that area.
- Talk to a consultant who is expert in that weakest area?
- Employ a professional business coach?

It can be hard to have confidence that any plan is exactly right. This is a fundamental challenge of leadership. How to proceed when there is uncertainty. The future is rarely predictable. Sometimes, it is like feeling your way forward in the dark. You can never be fully certain what lays ahead until you get there.

You must do your best to plan using the information you have. Further information will reveal itself as you get closer to your goal, allowing you to adapt your plans as you proceed. As your experience develops you will gain more insight as to what to expect on the same or similar routes in the future.

In the end, you need to take a deep breath, have courage, and give it your best attempt.

FitBiz example
Returning to Sarah's FitBiz, she identified three key areas to improve when creating her groupings:
1 Managing staff and improving operational efficiency
2 Management accounts and better planning
3 Overall improved marketing

In the process of understanding these areas, Sarah asked herself, 'What is missing that would make these a 10?' Using this thinking, Sarah came up with the following three sub-goals for her first area:

> *1. Managing staff and improving operational efficiency*
> *i) Identify key tasks to delegate*
> *ii) Train staff in new tasks*
> *iii) Weekly follow-ups to check delegated tasks*

Sarah's rationale is as follows:

i) Identify key tasks to delegate
If Sarah wants to improve her operations, she has to recognise she can not do it all herself. She needs to enrol her staff to help. For this, she needs to identify the key tasks to delegate. By applying the 80/20 rule, she may find that 20% of her tasks need to remain in her control. The remaining 80% she can delegate. Or 20% of her tasks take up 80% of her time and she should seek to delegate as many of these as she can.

ii) Train staff in new tasks
Sarah recognises that if she is to delegate, she needs to train her staff in a structured manner. If she dumps everything on them at once, it could result in chaos, risking her taking back the tasks and again doing them all herself! She needs to decide the order and sequence in which to deliver her training that will be quickest and easiest, with least risk to the business, and give her the greatest rewards in free time.

iii) Weekly follow-ups to check delegated tasks
Having trained and delegated to her staff, she will need to check they are doing those tasks correctly. Until she is confident in their ability, she should schedule follow-up sessions; first weekly, then monthly, then quarterly.

Sarah continued this process, prioritising her next two areas:

> ## 2. Improved financial performance
> ### i) Annual budget for profit
> ### ii) Monthly analysis of profit & loss statements
> ### iii) Research and implement new accounts software

Sarah's rationale is as follows:

i) Annual budget for profit
Looking at Sarah's low profit score, she knew this was a reflection of her high investment in the business that year, as well as a lack of a proper

budget. Rough figures had been considered, but not in any detail. Going forward, she needs good estimates of her revenue and costs to ensure a better profit. This needs to be her first priority.

ii) Monthly analysis of profit & loss statements
Sarah has accurate cash flow projections and up-to-date bookkeeping. She also knows her sales targets. Armed with her new budget, she now needs to produce a monthly profit and loss report to review her progress against her targets for profit.

iii) Research and implement new accounts software
The last stage in Sarah's financial plans will be to introduce new accounting software. The system they use currently does not easily produce the reports she needs. Once in place, Sarah knows they will benefit from a better system. As this will take time to implement, she plans this for the latter part of the year, once her staff are taking on more of her workload.

3. Overall improved marketing
i) Structured marketing plan
ii) Fortnightly reviews of marketing actions
iii) Research and implement a CRM system

Sarah's rationale is as follows:

i) Structured marketing plan
Sarah knows FitBiz has an ad hoc approach to marketing. They are clear on their marketing fundamentals: their competitive advantage, market, message and media. But this has never translated into a structured marketing plan with consistent actions. It doesn't need to be complicated, but is important to put in place.

ii) Fortnightly reviews of marketing actions
If Sarah's team work to create a simple marketing plan, it makes sense that her next sub-goal is to review their progress against it on a regular basis. This would ensure actions are being taken, and that they measure and improve the success of their results.

iii) Research and implement a CRM system

Sarah knows that if they are to improve their marketing, they will need to build their list of contacts and keep a better record of enquiries. They also want to schedule regular contact with certain clients between sessions and introduce a referral programme. This will be more efficient with a proper CRM (customer relationship management) system. Sarah did consider this as her first sub-goal, but decided to get her improved marketing underway first.

FitBiz's draft annual priorities

Sarah's first attempt at her plan looks like this:

FitBiz Example - Annual Priorities 2OXX

1). Improved Leadership & Operational Efficiency

    i. Identify key tasks to delegate

    ii. Train staff in new tasks

    iii. Weekly follow-ups on new tasks

2). Financial Performance for Profit

    i. Create an annual budget for profit

    ii. Schedule monthly analysis of P&Ls

    iii. Research + implement accounts software

3). Structured & Consistent Marketing

    i. Create a simple marketing plan

    ii. Fortnightly reviews of markeing actions

    iii. Research and introduce CRM system

To decide if these are right, Sarah should ask herself:

- Will these priorities and sub-goals move the business forward in the right direction this year?
- Will this really make the changes I am looking for?

If the answer is no, or not far enough, Sarah needs to reconsider and create a second draft, and repeat these questions, until she has a set of priorities and that she is happy with. When these finally feel right, Sarah has a list of priorities and sub-goals which form a simple plan for the year ahead.

Quarterly Sub Goals and Monthly Tasks

To ensure that your annual priorities and sub-goals get achieved, you need to break them down again into shorter timeframes. Quarterly sub-goals provide a good focus. Detailed plans beyond that timeframe often get derailed. Although it is important to have a rough sense of what will be required further down the line, those plans can become fine-tuned as you get closer.

Quarterly goals can be created in the same manner as your annual priorities, but with additional information. This includes:

- A more detailed task list
- The name/initial of the person accountable for each task
- A date to start or complete each task

In the same way, you can then create a task list for the next month or week.

To develop your annual priorities into quarterly goals we are using MetalFabs Ltd as an example. Their first annual priority is similar to Sarah's, but they are taking a more detailed approach, as laid out below.

MetalFabs quarterly goals example

MetalFabs - Quarterly Goals
Q1 (Jan-Mar 20XX)

	by Whom / When	
Managing staff and improving operational efficiency		
i. Identify key tasks that drive the business	AB	
a) Team briefing to discuss intentions		21/1
b) Process mapping to identify key processes		28/1
c) Time Management analysis of major tasks		7/2
d) Create shortlist of key tasks to improve		14/2
ii. Regular review meetings of key tasks & improvements	BC	
a) Create agenda		14/2
b) Schedule meetings in team diary		14/2
c) Confirm dates and intentions with team		14/2
d) Run 1st meeting		21/2
iii. Quarterly staff appraisals (+ identify training needs)	AB	tbc
a) Review job descriptions	AB	
- ensure staff aligned + accountable with key tasks		
b) Review appraisals system		
c) Complete first appraisals all key staff	AB/BC	

Advanced Goal Setting and SMART Goals

To this point, you have worked in a simplified manner to produce a simple plan with priorities and goals. Remember, even well established businesses fail to act because their plans are too complex. But if you already use a more advanced system and are happy with it, then stay with what works for you.

Planning is not an easy skill to master. Even the most experienced leaders find this exercise intellectually challenging. So remember, with all skill development, keep working at it and it will improve.

As you develop in confidence, your planning can become more comprehensive. To do so, here are some concepts of advanced planning that will help you.

SMART goals

SMART goals are:

Specific – a clearly defined area for improvement

Measurable – an agreed indicator of progress

Assignable – a person made accountable

Realistic – can be achieved with the agreed resources

Time-related – linked to agreed timescales

Why do you need smart goals? Have you ever said to yourself, 'I am going to get fit this year'? And if so, did you succeed? Approximately 80% of people who make New Year's resolutions to get fit drop off by the second week of February. Gyms typically sell memberships with the expectation that a mere 18% of people will use them throughout the year.

Why do so many people fail? Because they did not actually set a goal. What they did was make a wish. Their wish was just a vague notion of what they wanted, with few or no specifics. A SMART goal creates actions that will be measurable, so that it becomes clear whether you are succeeding or failing.

A specific goal about getting fit might include measures of losing X amount of weight, or being able to increase a running distance by Y. It might specify going to the gym on Mondays, Wednesdays and Fridays for Z hours training time, with the allocated exercises and performance targets on each day.

*A SMART goal reminds you of exactly what you need to do,
and allows you to measure if you have achieved it.*

The art of effective planning is to consider the most pertinent facts; to clarify your own thinking and to engage your team. You need to be thorough, but avoid creating confusion or mental overload to ensure you think clearly. These questions highlight mission critical information required for most projects:

- **What:** What is it?
  - The central idea, physical object, the objective.
- **Why:** Why is this important?
  - What is your reason for being interested or involved.
- **How:** How will you do it?
  - What is your method of making this work?
- **Who:** Who should be involved?
  - Who are the key people to enrol for this to work, internally and externally?
- **Where:** Where will this take place?
  - Where are the boundaries or limits of your project, by geographic location, product lines, departments, clients, markets, demographics etc?
- **When:** When do key events need to happen?
  - What dates do you need to work to and which are mission critical?
- **How Much:** To what degree should we do this?
  - How much will you be putting in? What are the quantities involved in whatever units are the most relevant; be it people, time, money, products, services.
- **At What Cost:** What will this cost you or gain you?
  - What resources will be required; money, time, energy, emotions, relationships, and what will you gain in return? Is it worth it?
- **At What Risk:** What are the greatest risks involved?
  - What do you risk most if you do this, or don't do this?
  - What do you risk if you fail or if you succeed?

Strategy template

These mission critical questions have been incorporated into this template, used for thinking through your strategic priorities in detail:

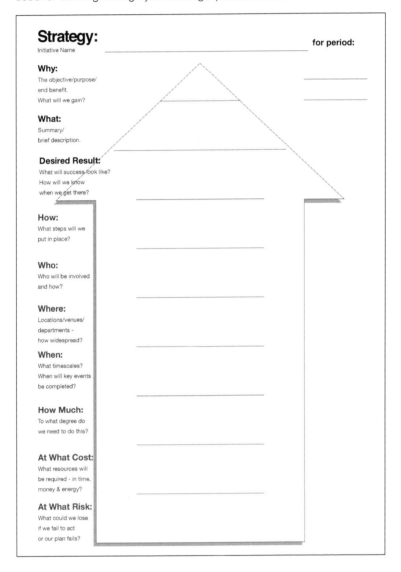

Strategy:

Initiative Name   **for period:**

Why:
The objective/purpose/
end benefit.
What will we gain?

What:
Summary/
brief description.

Desired Result:
What will success look like?
How will we know
when we get there?

How:
What steps will we
put in place?

Who:
Who will be involved
and how?

Where:
Locations/venues/
departments -
how widespread?

When:
What timescales?
When will key events
be completed?

How Much:
To what degree do
we need to do this?

At What Cost:
What resources will
be required - in time,
money & energy?

At What Risk:
What could we lose
if we fail to act
or our plan fails?

MetalFabs strategy example

This example shows how MetalFabs used the template to test the validity of an annual priority:

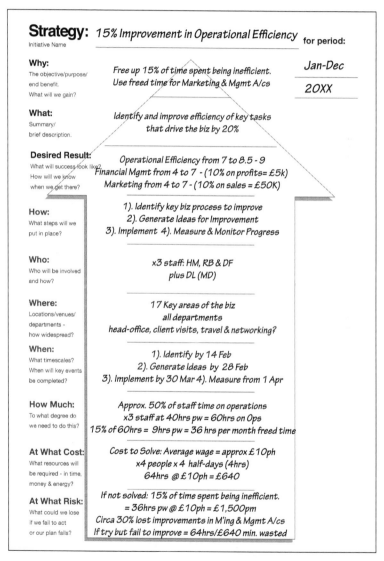

Strategy: _15% Improvement in Operational Efficiency_ **for period:**
Initiative Name

Why:
The objective/purpose/
end benefit.
What will we gain?

Free up 15% of time spent being inefficient.
Use freed time for Marketing & Mgmt A/cs

Jan-Dec
_20XX_

What:
Summary/
brief description.

Identify and improve efficiency of key tasks
that drive the biz by 20%

Desired Result:
What will success look like?
How will we know
when we get there?

Operational Efficiency from 7 to 8.5 - 9
Financial Mgmt from 4 to 7 - (10% on profits= £5k)
Marketing from 4 to 7 - (10% on sales = £50K)

How:
What steps will we
put in place?

1). Identify key biz process to improve
2). Generate Ideas for Improvement
3). Implement 4). Measure & Monitor Progress

Who:
Who will be involved
and how?

x3 staff: HM, RB & DF
plus DL (MD)

Where:
Locations/venues/
departments -
how widespread?

17 Key areas of the biz
all departments
head-office, client visits, travel & networking?

When:
What timescales?
When will key events
be completed?

1). Identify by 14 Feb
2). Generate Ideas by 28 Feb
3). Implement by 30 Mar 4). Measure from 1 Apr

How Much:
To what degree do
we need to do this?

Approx. 50% of staff time on operations
x3 staff at 40hrs pw = 60hrs on Ops
15% of 60hrs = 9hrs pw = 36 hrs per month freed time

At What Cost:
What resources will
be required - in time,
money & energy?

Cost to Solve: Average wage = approx £10ph
x4 people x 4 half-days (4hrs)
64hrs @ £10ph = £640

At What Risk:
What could we lose
if we fail to act
or our plan fails?

If not solved: 15% of time spent being inefficient.
= 36hrs pw @ £10ph = £1,500pm
Circa 30% lost improvements in M'ing & Mgmt A/cs
If try but fail to improve = 64hrs/£640 min. wasted

There are many ways to think through your projects or plans. Experiment and find what works best for you.

The Value of Thinking Things Through

This helps you to:
- Evaluate the benefits of a project. Is it really worthwhile this year?
- Prevent costly mistakes that could have been avoided
- Pre-empt issues and save time by planning ahead
- Consider the true extent, and boundaries, of your project
- Ensure the right people are involved

At what cost?

With questions such as 'At what cost?', it is tempting to give answers such as, 'It's just my time', and to leave it there. Instead, think through how many hours would be involved for the task and multiply that by the approximated hourly rate. With a full-time member of staff, earning approximately £20k per annum and working approximately 40 hours a week, the sum would be:

£20k ÷ 52 ÷ 40 = £9.61 per hour

If you estimate that they would spend two hours a week on your project over three months, then you would calculate:

2 hours per week x 3 months x 4 weeks per month
2 x 3 x 4 = 24 hours
24 hours x £9.61ph = £231

Very approximately for the project:

The cost of their time = £231

If you had a member of staff on £50k pa, working on the same project, working four hours per week, the cost of their time would look like this:

£50k ÷ 52 ÷ 40 = £24ph x 48 hours (project time) = £1,152 cost of time

Obviously there are other costs to employing a member of staff such as National Insurance and pension contributions to take into account. However, this quick calculation gives you an approximation of the cost or benefit of them being involved. If the project were to save you £500 pa, but cost you £1,152 in time to improve it, then clearly it would not be worth your while. You may decide that it would be cheaper to have the problem outsourced or an automated solution implemented.

What is your desired result?

You need to be specific about the benefit of the project. For example, it would be easy to write 'improved marketing'. If you are specific you tell a better story.

With the MetalFabs example, they want to improve their operational efficiency to free up time for marketing. Even if they start with a wild guess and assume that a 30% increase in their marketing effectiveness may lead to a 10% increase in sales, they could write:

30% increase in marketing effectiveness = 10% increase in sales
10% increase in sales = £50k

If they know that they operate at about 10% net profit, then they could conclude that:

10% increase in sales = £50k
£50k revenue at 10% = £5k increase net profit

They have calculated the cost of staff time for the project as £640, so the simplified financial story looks like this:

£640 investment in staff time = increase in profits @ £5k pa

The question now for MetalFabs is whether or not this is worthwhile return on their time and effort compared to any other option.

Admittedly, these are only crude figures. But remember, one of the greatest barriers to planning is not planning at all because accurate figures are not available or would take too long to collate. If the crude story looks good, if the project appears worthwhile with approximate figures, then it is worth further consideration and a more accurate review. If the crude story looks unattractive the project can be rejected with no further waste of time.

If a project involves large amounts of time and money, then you would definitely want to test the accuracy of your figures, before taking any action. Also, some businesses do not have exact figures to work with even if they wanted to. This process highlights the kind of information you need to start recording so that it becomes available to you in the future.

If all of this is new to you, then do not be disheartened. You are not alone. Developing clarity with your business information starts with a mindset shift. This comes from the practice of thinking through your plans and forcing yourself to make assumptions. The more you do this, the more you will become confident in the type of information you need to record in more detail.

Start Your Planning Cycle

Whatever your current level of planning ability, novice or expert, use this process to raise your game. Pay attention to what works best for you. Remember, practice and repetition makes perfect.

By creating better plans, you will be creating better targets. As you have better targets you will need to put in place the measurements or KPIs (key performance indicators) to track your progress towards them. As you put these measurements in place, you will develop better business information. And so in turn, with better information, your future planning will develop in a cycle of continuous improvement.

Whether you feel anxious or motivated take action now!

- Create your plans for the year ahead – however simple or complex
- Work to a higher standard than you have previously
- Decide what measurements you need to track your progress
- Review your progress often and at agreed intervals
- Celebrate your progress along the way
- If you get stuck, decide what action may help with the block
- Above all – enjoy the journey

In the next section you are encouraged to test your business knowledge in greater depth. It will help you identify what you may want to improve next, or where you may need to learn more. As with all knowledge, there is no limit to how far you can go. But remember, knowledge only becomes wisdom when blended with experience and understanding. Make sure you put your current plans into action so your knowledge becomes real.

What you have learned

- Avoid a major planning mistake
  - Resist attempting too much detail too soon
- The value of:
  - The 80/20 rule. What will create the most valuable gain for the least effort?
  - The power of threes. Easy to remember and focus on
  - Strategic *vs* day-to-day goals. System vs incremental change
- Start with your annual priorities, the big picture end goals
- Break them down to create your:
  - Quarterly goals
  - Monthly tasks

Tips

- Be prepared to create several drafts
- Refer to your work in the previous two chapters
- It is better to write something than nothing
- You can revisit your plans – improve them in stages
- If new to planning, remember, your plans will become better with practice

Required actions from this chapter

- Use your Business Jet Engine® diagram with your marked priority areas
- Develop your thinking into written plans by writing:
  - Three annual priorities
  - Three subgoals for each priority
  - A plan for your first quarter
  - A task-list for your first month

In the next section

- Fine tune your knowledge of The Business Jet Engine® using:
  - the summary concepts for each area
  - the advanced diagnostic questions

Section 3

Fine Tuning
for maximum performance

This is the section for keeping your Business Jet Engine® tuned so you can climb faster and fly higher. This section will increasingly help you refine and improve your knowledge and business, over time.

Here you will learn:

- Key concepts to strengthen each area of your business
- Advanced diagnostic questions for your Business Jet Engine® model

These will help you:

- Ensure you have essential frameworks in place for each area of your business
- Guide your own future development and learning

Including more involved concepts of:

● Business planning
● KPIs and measuring and monitoring your progress

Return to this section repeatedly to continually improve your knowledge and the performance of your business. Once you have the basic frameworks in place for each area, you can use the diagnostic questions to direct your development and learning.

The aim of this section is to

- Explain key concepts in each part of The Business Jet Engine® model
- Highlight gaps in your knowledge
- Help you identify what you need to learn about next
- Help you identify what you need to improve next

Tips

- Decide how best to use this section. See *Three possible approaches* in this section introduction:
  - Quick insight
  - To be more thorough
  - If you are unsure how to improve a weak area

Actions

- Read the relevant chapters or sub-headings
- Score yourself using the advanced diagnostic questions
- Decide what you need to develop and how you will do it

Using This Section

Previous sections have helped you see where you may be stuck on the runway. By seeing your business as a system, you have identified what is missing, put plans in place and are ready for takeoff.

You should now know:

- The current state of your business
- Where your business is weak and strong
- Your three top strategic priorities for the year ahead
- Your business' quarterly goals and monthly tasks

The work you have done so far has been based on your current level of business experience and knowledge. This has been important to get you started, so you have immediate plans and actions to focus on for today and tomorrow. But whatever your level of experience, there is always more to learn or an area that you have probably neglected. If you are a novice entrepreneur, you will want to fine tune your business as fast as possible and get lift off. If you are a seasoned entrepreneur, with your aircraft up in the air and flying well, you will want to make sure your aircraft is at maximum altitude and cruising speed.

Whichever point you are at, the key question is, what do you work on next?

This section as a diagnostic tool

The greatest value of this section is in the diagnostic questions. These are dispersed throughout each chapter, preceded by the concepts my clients find most useful. However, these concepts are not exhaustive. This book is not intended to be a business manual. That would be a different book, and would be much larger and more complex in size and scope. This book is about helping you identify quickly where you are weak and strong, and putting plans in place to strengthen those areas.

This section takes the process we used in Section 2 to a more advanced level. It is designed to be a simple but powerful diagnostic tool. By giving a quick overview of the major business areas, and then identifying the areas that next need fine-tuning, you can get your own Business Jet Engine® flying at maximum efficiency and performance.

Three possible approaches
Approach one – if you want a quick insight

Go straight to the diagnostic questions, omitting the overview text on each area, and score yourself against each question. If you do not understand a question, you are probably weak in that area and should be giving yourself a low score.

For each section, you can establish an average score. By comparing scores for each area it will become clear what you need to develop next.

Approach two – if you want to be more thorough

Read the summary text for each area. Then having tested your own knowledge against that area, you can apply your scores. Again, calculate your average score for each area, and by comparison, identify what you need to develop next.

Approach three – if you are unsure how to improve a weak area

If you have identified an area of your business that is weak, but you are unsure what to do next, go to that specific area and read the summary. If the summary highlights what you are missing, then focus on developing your skill and knowledge in that area. If you have all the summary concepts in place, then use the diagnostic questions for more in-depth analysis of what to improve.

The value of this section for a novice or seasoned entrepreneur

If you are a novice entrepreneur, there will be many areas where you need to develop. If you are a seasoned business person, you will no doubt find there are areas where you are more expert than this book. If you have many years in business, I would expect that to be the case. However it is unlikely that you will be strong in every single area of business.

Business leaders tend to build their businesses reflecting their own strengths. A leader strong on finance will build a company that is driven largely by financial factors. A leader strong on innovation and design, will tend to build their company based on product development, whilst possibly being less focused on finance. A leader strong on people and interpersonal skills will tend to build their business by hiring a strong team and building business connections.

The risk for any leader, novice or experienced, is that they will be exposed by a blindspot, an area of their business in which they are not fully aware of all the opportunities or risks. Whatever your level, you can use this section to assess each business area. If you feel you are comprehensively strong in every area, the chances are your team may not share your breadth of knowledge. This section can be used to develop the business knowledge of your team.

From experience, I find novice business owners tend to score themselves optimistically at first. This is both appropriate and to be expected. They are less aware of what they do not know or are missing. With experience, they realise how much they do not yet have in place and score themselves more harshly.

Remain positive. By applying the diagnostic approach in this section, you can then plan the order and sequence of your own development in a realistic way.

CHAPTER SEVEN

The Heart of Your Business Jet Engine®
the hard mechanics

Your engine's foundations are pieces of sheet and machined metal, pipes and tubes, electronics and cabling, bearings, oil and lubricants. All of this is the hard engineering that goes into the engine, makes everything revolve, and powers flight. Your plane wouldn't fly without an engine to create thrust, and so it is with business. Your product, customer service and operations are where it all starts, right at the heart of your business.

Your Product

At the outset of building an engine, you start with the hard-engineered parts that make up the bulk of it. The casing, rotors, shafts, compressors, turbines, nozzles, fans and blades. These are the foundational parts that do the work of compressing air and fuel and turning them into power and thrust.

Just as these major parts are the starting point of any engine, so the product of your business, the problems you solve for your clients, are your starting point. This is all the hard stuff that takes the stresses and strains. This is the raw challenge you have: solving problems for your clients. Your product can be tested to destruction so it must perform well in their eyes if you want to do well. You have to deliver on your promises. The greater the perceived value of the problems you solve, the more you get paid. If you want handsome rewards, you must excel at solving what is valued most and you need to solve that problem for them better than anybody else.

The first step in solving problems is to ensure that you really understand the problem. To do that you need to have in-depth discussions with the people involved. You need to study the problems to see what causes the greatest challenges.

You need to check how customers currently solve those problems and understand how this could be improved. How far are their current solutions from their ideal? Can they even imagine what an ideal solution would look like? Are you able to imagine a solution that would cause them to be amazed?

The better you solve their problems and the greater the perceived value of your solutions – the more you can charge!

Competitive advantage – *USPs, differentiation, core competence*

There is little point in providing a product or service that is average. It makes it hard to stand out from the crowd and attract a sale. Without a sale, you only have a dream, not a business.

It is hard to build a loyal customer base if you are no better than everybody else. It is costly in time, money and energy to attract new business. Once you have that business you want your customers to stay with you; to buy from you again and again and recommend you. In order to do that you need to do something unique/better/different that your customers truly value. This requires understanding a few subtly different concepts that relate to this.

USPs

A unique selling point means that in your sales and marketing activities you highlight something that nobody else is talking about. It does not guarantee that the competition does not offer the same, it just means that they are not making a feature of it.

Differentiation

Means that you *do* offer something better and different. This could be a better product, service, customer service, costs, people, brand recognition or reputation, features, functions, after sales back-up, warranty, upgrade facility, or some other *unique element* which your customers truly want/need/value.

Now this is great to have but if your competitors can see what you are doing, and see that it is working for you, then they can simply copy you. At that point, you have essentially been their R&D department at your expense.

Competitive Advantage

This is where you can really come into your own. Competitive advantage means that whatever you do that is uniquely different is also extremely hard to copy. If you are hard to copy then it is hard for the competition to catch up with you overnight. This will give you a competitive edge.

To really have this advantage, your point of difference is normally underpinned by the way you have invested time, money or energy, and your competitors will have to make similar investments to match you. This might mean that you have invested in training, development, more in-depth product or customer research, better technology, systems and processes, more highly researched and analysed sales and marketing, legal protection such as copyright, trademarks, patents etc.

These kinds of underlying investments can set you apart and over time give you an advantage that is hard to replicate. But remember, it must also deliver something truly valued by your clients.

For a difference to last it must be hard to imitate.

Core Competences

These are the things you do better than anyone else, that are at the heart of who you are and what you do. They typically pass four tests to qualify:

- They add value to the client
- They are not widely available
- They are hard to copy
- You are well organised with systems and processes to exploit your key difference

If you have competitive advantage, this is the start to building a strong business. If you doubt you have it then list:

- What problems you solve for your clients
- How you add value to them by solving it
- What you have invested time, money and energy into, to deliver that solution
- How the above makes you unique from your competition

If you still do not think you have it, what could you do that others would find difficult, but which is relatively easy for you?

Product Diagnostic Questions

How well do you:

Product

Understand your customers' problems and challenges?

Clearly define the problem(s) your customers really
want solved?

Know what your clients really value?

Know what they would be willing to pay for a truly
ideal solution?

Know what your clients score your solution to
their problems?

Competitive advantage

Ensure you have a product your customers cannot
get elsewhere?

Ensure you have a product they truly value and will pay for?

Ensure it is hard for others to copy or improve on
your solution?

Clearly identify and develop your core competence and
competitive advantage?

Organise yourself to exploit your key difference?

Clearly and simply communicate your core competence
to your customers?

Customer Service – the bearings and lubricants

With our jet engine metaphor, customer service is like the bearings, oils and lubricants that let your engine move at great speed under pressure. Customer service prevents your engine, your customers or you from getting too hot, stuck or exploding. Great customer service keeps everything cool, with your engine spinning sweetly.

A business is only a business if it has customers and it is far easier to build a business if you retain the ones you work so hard to win. To retain customers, you must be able to meet their needs, even great demands. They need to feel cared about, even loved – which is customer service.

Creating customer delight

Customers also have a great deal of choice as to where they can go for products and services, so are increasingly less loyal. They want great value, supplied quickly from wherever is easiest. To counteract so much choice and keep your customers coming back you must do more than sell products and services.

People buy based on how they feel, so to attract customers, you must also sell an amazing experience. That means thinking beyond traditional good customer service. This is now the norm, and is expected. You need to deliver a 'Wow!' service. A service that is unexpected. A service that is exceptional, stands out and is memorable for all the right reasons.

Consistency of brand

You also need to deliver that Wow! service *consistently* at every point of contact the customer has with you, from beginning to end, each time they deal with you, including online and offline. These points of contact are your brand, not just your logo as some people believe.

Frequent points of contact/customer experience include:
- Your logo and branding, in all locations
- Signage and how easily they can find you
- All forms of communication including phone, emails, social media and face-to-face

- Understanding what you offer
- Finding what they need
- Query and complaint handling
- Being able to purchase your products
- After sales and service
- Repeat business and follow-up contact

All these points of contact add to how they feel treated by you and your staff, and whether or not they feel cared about and loved. Or whether they feel like just another number on your financial spreadsheets.

To match or exceed expectations, you need to do what you promise or more. Deliver sooner, at a lower cost. Solve more than was hoped for. If you can deliver something extra as well, a sprinkle of wow, you have a great chance of keeping your customers.

Failure to deliver on your promises results in unhappy customers who will tell others. With social media and our inter-connected world your tarnished reputation will quickly be spread, taking far more to repair it than protect it in the first place. Your most loyal customers may even defend you if you delight them consistently. And how you repair a one-off mistake can also build loyalty if you show how much you care.

Delivering great service relies on three things:
- Staff and your business culture being customer focused
- Customer focus being embedded into everything you do
- Reinforcing and rewarding customer friendly behaviour

Creating a customer focused culture would include looking after first impressions, managing the greeting of customers, using and remembering names, asking great questions to develop rapport, developing a lasting impression, following-up on enquiries or quotes, after sales service, pro-active re-engagement with clients, pro-actively seeking accurate and objective customer feedback.

This can be aided by staff training and recruiting those with a natural love of working with people, as opposed to recruiting on a product based skill set. The culture can be rewarded and reinforced by acknowledging and praising great behaviours in the moment, and by acknowledgement through award schemes and mentions in company communications.

Service as sales, sales as service

In addition to customers feeling loved and cared about, this concept links customer care with the important act of selling, or more appropriately, helping people to buy. Your potential customers have a pain, a problem, a need, a want, a desire, and they are looking for someone to fix it. Helping them find what they need is central to making a sale.

This requires asking them about their needs and wants, which leads us on to the need for staff to have excellent product knowledge.

Customer service training and product knowledge

To truly help a customer solve their problems, you and your staff need to have an excellent understanding of what you can offer to meet those needs. This includes having an appropriate questioning process for under-standing your clients' wants, and excellent product knowledge to offer solutions without the client having to search or enquire elsewhere. Both of these may require training to ensure all staff are fully competent.

Implementing regular and well-structured customer service train-ing provides an environment where company values can be effectively communicated to all staff and embedded in their daily customer-facing tasks. This ensures your customers have a consistent and valuable experience no matter which staff member they deal with.

In addition, product knowledge training will improve the confidence of your staff. If they believe in what you do, their knowledge and confidence will create passion. And passion is a feeling most people want. A feeling which will transmit to your customers so they feel great about you.

Customer Service Diagnostic Questions

Customer delight and brand consistency

How well do you:

Create an experience that your customers think is Wow!?

Ensure your brand expresses that Wow!?

Consistently embody your brand across all areas of your business?

Maintain that experience at every point of contact?

Ensure your clients can find what they need?

Ensure your clients feel fully looked after and cared for?

Obtain accurate feedback of your clients' experience of you?

Customer service training and product knowledge

How well do your staff:

Ensure your clients feel helped, cared for and loved?

Show motivation and passion when helping customers?

Understand your customers and their deepest, most relevant needs?

Understand your products, and how they solve those client needs?

Feel fully competent in both your products and customer service processes?

Deal with client fears/objections when considering a purchase?

Ask for an order when appropriate?

Smooth Operations – the systems and processes that keep it all working

In our engine metaphor, we talked about the product of your business being like the hard-engineered parts such as the casing, rotors, shafts and blades. Alongside this, there are all the support systems that make everything co-ordinate, so you create the desired end result: a powerful thrust-producing engine.

All these have to work in a safe, efficient, repeatable and predictable manner to allow you to achieve flight. In a similar way, the operations of a business allow you to deliver your product or service, at the right quality, at the desired time as smoothly and predictably as possible.

Efficient and effective operations can give you a real competitive edge. When done well, they should save you time, money and energy, minimise your business risk and ultimately, and most importantly, ensure your customers receive the consistent experience they hope for.

For some businesses, their operations may be modest and simple. For example, a freelance graphic designer will have relatively straightforward procedures for acquiring a project, developing and delivering it. For other businesses, this can be a vast and complex arena and the major part of their work. This would be true for a global logistics company where concepts such as site-layout, package tracking and investment in infrastructure are major concerns absorbing significant proportions of time, money, material and energy. At this point, operations management becomes a discipline and science, and as discussed, a major source of competitive advantage in itself.

The basics of operations

Whether you deliver a product or service, the simplest way to think of operations is to imagine three parts. You have:

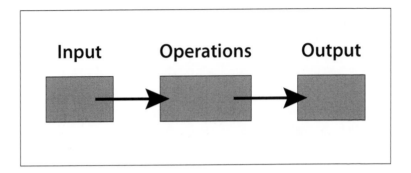

- **Inputs** – what comes in to your business
- **Operations** – what you do to those inputs to produce your outputs
- **Outputs** – what comes out at the other end that you sell

Operations is everything in the middle that turns your inputs into outputs, and most importantly, how well you do that to meet the demands of your customers. This depends on a variety of factors:

- **Volume** – the quantity of product or service required
- **Value** – how fully it solves your customers needs linked to what they will pay
- **Demand** – the quantity and timings of when it is wanted by the customer

The challenge of operations is to decide how to deliver this at the appropriate:

- **Consistency** – in a predictable manner
- **Quality** – to the expected standard
- **Reduction of Risk** – keeping threats to people and business at a minimum

The key to this is developing repeatable ways of doing things; your systems and processes.

Systems and process improvement

Systems and processes are key to growing any business. In fact, the more complex your business, the more important they become. Before going too far let us clarify what is meant by systems and processes.

The Oxford English Dictionary defines a *system* as:
* A set of things working together as parts of a mechanism or an inter-connecting network; a complex whole
* A set of principles or procedures according to which something is done; an organised scheme or method

And a *process* as:
* A series of actions or steps taken in order to achieve a particular end
* To deal with someone or something using an official procedure

A system or process will include the items or equipment you use, including physical layout, and the method or sequence by which you take action. In a manufacturing plant, this would include the layout of your machinery and the sequence with which goods flow through the factory.

Manufacturing would also need to link to another system, sales, to ensure that the correct goods are made as ordered by the customer. These also link to dispatch, to ensure they are correctly packed and delivered.

Common business systems include all the parts of The Business Jet Engine® from creating your product, right through to planning and monitoring progress.

Five benefits of systems and processes

They are:
* Efficient
* Effective
* Repeatable
* Teachable
* Allows for incremental improvement

1) Efficient, simplified, streamlined, maximises time

The first part of a good system is that it should be as simple and stream-lined as possible. Unnecessary parts or actions should be left out, reducing clutter and creating the fastest route to the end result, maximising time available for other work.

2) Effective, maximises quality, minimises risk and ensures desired results

The second part of a good system is that it produces the correct result. There is simply no purpose being efficient producing something that misses the mark. In addition, correcting errors or re-doing work is a costly exercise in any business, especially if the product has reached the customer.

An effective system should also minimise risk, especially where there is risk to health, wellbeing, client relations, brand reputation or business continuity. Effective systems ensure the desired quality and result are achieved with minimum risk.

3) Repeatable, reliable, consistent, predictable

The third part of a good system is that once it is working, you can simply 'rinse and repeat'. The process can be replicated to create the same result and extract the same benefit. Predictable results allow you to analyse the past and make more accurate plans for the future. Complex procedures, or those reliant on certain staff, may need to be documented.

4) Teachable

Once you have a system that is efficient, effective and repeatable, you can now teach it. If you can teach it, then you are no longer dependent on a few people who can make your system work. You can apply the power of people and efficiently scale that part of your business.

5) Incremental improvement

Also with a system that is repeatable, you can identify the areas that can be further improved. This is hard to do when your approach and results vary. There is no precedent with which to compare your changes. Repeatable systems allow you to trial new approaches and measure their success against current performance.

Ideally, every part of The Business Jet Engine® should be run as a systemised, teachable process.

However, with any business, you should start by identifying the handful of activities that cost you most time, money or energy or expose you to risk. From this shortlist, prioritise which activity to improve first and how long you can afford to spend on the improvement process.

From here, the key steps are:

- Ensure you have a performance measure for your current process, e.g. it currently takes 3 hours
- Decide what the new measure of success would look like, e.g. 2.5 hours
- Identify the key parts of the process
- Identify where problems occur most frequently
- Develop options to improve these problem areas
- Test and trial these options against your current process
- Refine and improve until your target measure is achieved
- If required, train staff in the new process
- If necessary, document the new process to ensure it is now followed

Many processes, with a little thought, can be improved simply by better:

- workflow, e.g. proximity/layout/location of equipment, materials or information
- labelling and storage
- checklists and/or documentation

Managing risk

In addition, improved operations should also consider how to manage risk. There are four main types of risk, but be aware, risk can occur in any area of your Business Jet Engine®:

- strategic, i.e. from competitors or a change in market conditions
- compliance, i.e failure to comply with legislation such as employment law
- financial, i.e. non-payment by a major client
- operational, i.e. a major supplier going out of business

To prepare for these eventualities, you need to:

1   Identify risks in your core business areas
2   Consider how to minimise or eliminate those risks
3   Create a plan, who should do what should a scenario occur
4   Ensure all relevant parties understand and agree with the plan
5   Review your plans at timely intervals

In summary, better systems and processes may require initial investment, but should pay dividends in allowing you to grow and scale your business based on efficient, effective, reliable and teachable systems, which can then be improved as necessary over time.

Operations Diagnostic Questions

How well do you:

Core Systems & Processes
Identify, implement, manage and monitor

Identify your mission critical systems and processes?

Ensure they are aligned with your organisation's objectives?

Ensure they are streamlined to maximise efficiency and quality?

Ensure they minimise cost and risk?

Document processes and train staff as appropriate?

Analyse and improve performance?

Apply efficient systems to all parts of your Business Jet Engine®?

Keep your operations strategy up to date?

Production, suppliers, stock and delivery

Monitor your suppliers' capabilities and performance?

Ensure you have the right stock levels at the right time and cost?

Hit agreed deadlines, especially compared to the competition?

Check that you have done what you planned for your customers?

Support Systems
Legal

Ensure all contracts and your business structure best serves you?

Protect and exploit your intellectual property?

Ensure you have the most appropriate commercial property
arrangements?

Risk management, health and safety, insurance and security

Assess the major risks to your business that could stop
   you working?

Develop contingency plans for high risk scenarios?

Embed plans to minimise downtime for each scenario?

Ensure compliance with legal requirements where appropriate?

Ensure staff are trained as required?

Ensure all necessary risks are insured?

Assess and implement solutions for your physical
   security needs?

Quality and environmental

Follow environmental best practice?

Ensure your environmental processes meet any regulatory
   requirements?

Review your performance against any
   standards or requirements?

IT and communication

Develop a cost effective IT strategy?

Ensure IT systems are protected against threats?

Maintain regular/timely off-site back-ups of all
   your systems and data?

CHAPTER EIGHT

Sales & Marketing Airflow
keeping the work flowing in

Air is an essential ingredient. Vast quantities are sucked in, compressed and finally ignited with fuel to create thrust. Typically, more than 99% air is mixed with less than 1% of fuel, and this is why a jet engine has its characteristic shape with massive air intakes.

This should be reflected in the shape of your business. If sales and marketing are like your air intake, a vast number of people must be made aware of your product or service. This is then compressed down through your marketing and customer sales journey, until a few are ready to buy, converting goods into the cash that powers your business.

Marketing and sales are such an important activity for any business that I am going to describe them in detail. For many SME businesses, sales and marketing are the key drivers of growth and deserve appropriate attention.

Marketing

What is marketing?
I like to define marketing as all that activities that keep you at the forefront of an existing or potential customer's mind until they are ready to make an enquiry.

Sales, by contrast, covers all the activities you employ once an enquiry has been made. Marketing is about attracting a fish to the hook. Once the fish has taken the bait, or the client made an enquiry, then that becomes sales. The two functions overlap, and sales staff may take on some activities defined as marketing. This is especially true when involved in new business development. Nonetheless, everything is clearer when you distinguish the two activities:

1 Attracting an enquiry = marketing
2 Converting an enquiry = sales

To remain at the forefront of your customer's mind, and attract an enquiry, what do you need to do? For this, four concepts are especially helpful:

1 The marketing pyramid
2 The customer sales journey
3 5 to 21 touches
4 Attract-nurture-convert

The marketing pyramid

The marketing pyramid is the foundation of any marketing activity. The pyramid shows the three principal factors that must be properly considered at the outset of any campaign.

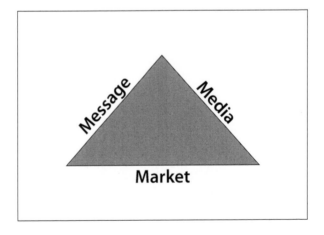

Your market – who is willing to pay for your solution

This is where you consider, in as much detail as possible, the people to whom you hope to sell, the product or service they are most likely to buy and why. The better you understand your market, the better your chance of meeting their needs.

Your message – what you solve and why it benefits them

This is what your market needs to hear for you to remain at the forefront of their awareness. For this, your market needs to understand who you are, the problems you can solve for them and the benefits of you doing so. Particularly if they are consumers, this needs to be described to them in words they would use themselves, not the language of your profession.

Your choice of media – where they engage with your message

This is where you choose from the hundreds of methods by which you get your message to your market, at a price you can afford. The challenge is to reach exactly the right people, your target audience, when they are most receptive to what you have to say. Ideally, you also need to be able to measure the effectiveness of your activity against a desired response.

The customer sales journey

Have you ever entered a shop where the sales assistant asks, 'Can I help you?'. Has your reaction been to say, 'No thanks, I'm just looking'? If so, beneath your reaction may be a fear of being pressured into a sale.

Most of us need to go through a process before we are ready to make a purchase. Otherwise, we can feel rushed and uncertain, and are likely to back away for fear of making a mistake. This process may happen over a few minutes, or many years. Typically, the more involved the purchase, the longer the timeframe required. This is the same for your potential clients. They may pass through stages such as:

- They don't have or care about the problem you solve
- They realise that they have the problem you solve
- They become curious, or start to research, how to solve their problem

- They make a short list of options to solve their problem
- They make a decision how to solve it
- Hopefully, they choose you and become your customer

Good marketeers realise they need to create messages
that appeal to their market at each stage of the process.

These messages will be clearly different depending on the stage.

For example, at the 'don't know they have the problem' stage, the message may be purely informative, such as 'Did you know, one in four men over thirty has low testosterone? Download our fact sheet for more information'. At the decision-making stage, the message may be, 'Buy your testosterone booster today and get an extra course free. Click here to purchase'. The second message would be wasted on someone who is not yet engaged by the offer.

Good marketeers also recognise that as customers move towards a purchase along their journey, they ask themselves key questions. These need to be addressed through good messaging which offers customers reassurance that you are the right person for the job.

- Who are you? Do I like you? Do I trust you?
- What problems do you solve? Do I have those problems?
- Would I want you to solve those problems for me?
- Is there another person or solution I would prefer to solve this for me?
- What is the risk if I use you?
- What if I wait? Am I ready to decide?

Typically, the more complex the problem and the higher the sums of money involved, the longer the process will take. Most people spend longer buying a car than they do choosing a new toothbrush, though bear in mind, some people spend months agonising over the choice of a new toothbrush! Most consultants know it can take them up to three years to win a major new client. Even if their first contact was positive, they may need to maintain gentle contact over a long period of time until that client is ready to work with them.

5 to 21 touches to a sale

Each moment of contact can be called a *touch*. You make contact with their awareness in some form; via an advert, an article, social media post, a letter, phone call, sales visit, a networking lunch, a round of golf. Each of these touches helps reconnect you, in their mind, as the most attractive solution to their problem as their need to solve that problem increases.

It may take between 5 and 21 touches to make a sale. Many businesses underestimate this, and their marketing activities fall short.

I have seen business people give up on a networking group, because after two meetings, they didn't make a sale. Members who remained committed to the group developed trusted relationships that eventually led to sales or referrals. This is true for most types of marketing. A one-off article in a magazine is unlikely to generate sales, compared to a series of articles in the same magazine, produced consistently over time.

The ideal is that your marketing messages are timed to suit your potential client's situation as they move along their sales journey. This is hard to achieve without close contact, hence the need for a sales representative who attempts to maintain contact with a prospect until they are ready to make a purchase.

Online, businesses track you, observing what you are interested in and tempting you onto the next stage towards making a purchase. If you have signed up to a mailing list, automated sequenced email campaigns can prompt you towards a sale. If you don't have insights provided by online tracking or a sales representative, you need research to create content which appeals to your customers at approximated stages in their sales journey.

Attract, nurture, convert – the three stage objective

The customer sales journey is useful as a concept and important to understand. To create more specific actions, it can be simplified into three objectives, expressed as:

The attract phase

The objective of the attract phase is to build your list of potential customers and gain contact information through which you can communicate or engage with them directly. This might include:

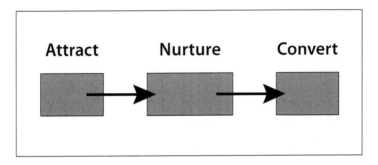

- Email, postal address or phone number
- They subscribe to social media you control such as:
  - newsletters, blogs, social media pages, forums

You offer them something they value for free or at very low cost, and in exchange by 'signing-up' they give permission for an ongoing relationship with you. This is sometimes called *Content*, *Inbound* or *Attraction Marketing*.

Your free or low-cost offer may include:

- Any form of information or product awareness
- Free events, taster experiences, product trials or demonstrations
- Videos that people want to watch and share

There is no fixed formula other than to ask yourself, 'What would my potential audience be most interested in for low cost or free, so they agree to a relationship with me?'. When built carefully, your list of people contains a proportion of future customers equating to your future profit, making list-building a high value activity.

The nurture phase

With clients now signed-up to your list, the objective is develop and nurture a relationship with them. For people to buy from you, they need to know you, like you and trust you to solve their problems. They also have to want what you offer, and be ready to pay for it, which can take time.

In order to develop the relationship, you can deepen their experience of you and your expertise. You want to demonstrate the benefits of buying from you, bearing in mind that many audiences will be turned off by a hard sell. This might include offering variations of your free or low-cost offer from the attract stage. It may be a more in-depth experience. Or you can demonstrate your expertise through quality information, giving them knowledge and insight. You can also help develop their trust in you by sharing case studies, showing end results backed up with client testimonials.

The converting phase

Having deepened your relationship with your list, the objective here is to create your first and subsequent sales. This separates those who are simply interested in you, and those who will buy from you. If a customer buys from you once, however low the cost or your profit margin, the chances are they will buy from you again.

Some people on your list will be forever interested in you but never actually make a purchase. The key is to make intelligent decisions whether or not you persist with them, but more importantly, to focus your activities on those ready and willing to make a first purchase.

Having made their first convincing purchase, you are better placed to offer them products again. This may be a repeat of their first purchase (repeat sales), such as more ink cartridges if you've supplied them before, or higher value products or add-ons (up-selling & cross-selling), such as a new printer, or an attachment for the one they bought last year.

Linking your marketing plan to your business plans

Answers to these questions need to be linked to your business plan and financial goals, covered in more detail in the Strategic Planning section.

In simple terms, to choose your best marketing approach, you have to know how many customers you need for your business goals. Do you need to acquire customers in their 10s, 100s, or 1,000s? Finding ten high-value clients will probably require a much more personal and bespoke approach, with personal contact where possible, compared to trying to attract thousands of new customers. For example, why create a complex online marketing strategy when your ten ideal prospects all frequent your local golf-club? You need to ask, how many clients do you need in what time frame to reach your financial targets? For each product group or client type, you can make a simplified equation to express this:

10 new clients per month x 12 months = 120 new clients per annum

If each client has an estimated spend per annum of approximately £1,000:

10 x 12 x £1k = £120k new sales target

Repeat this for each product group or client type, whichever best suits your business model. Use average figures and keep it simple if you have not done this before. I am surprised how many businesses fail to make simple targets but forge ahead with vague growth plans of 'just get more clients' and ad-hoc marketing activities that do not match the type or number of clients required.

What is your budget? What can you afford to spend to gain a customer? Compare what you invest with the potential long-term return per customer. Most people market only based on the return from the first sale.

Consider, what is an average customer worth to you over 30 days, annually and their lifetime. If your typical client spends £1k with you each year, and on average remains a client for five years, then:

£1k x 5 years = £5k

The average lifetime value of this type of client is £5k. On this basis, it may be worth spending several hundred pounds in sales and marketing to gain a similar client. Alternatively, if you run a sweet shop, and your average customer spends only £300 over three years, you wouldn't want to spend £300 to acquire that customer. This allows you to think through how much you could justify spending to gain each new client, against what your cashflow can afford.

Having thought through the three sides of the marketing triangle, you should:

- Create a marketing plan that is simple for you to follow
- Spend as much as you can afford
- Spend to stand out
- Outspend your competition
- Demonstrate by giving value before attempting to sell
- Develop a lifelong relationship
- Decide how to measure and analyse your results
- Test and improve your results over time

Marketing Diagnostic Questions

Strategy/Marketing Planning

How well do you:

Align your product or service with your long term business vision, mission and values?

Identify your short term (one or two year) business and sales goals?

Decide your marketing budget, aligned with your financial plans, for the year?

Research the market/need/demand for your product or service?

Research what customers truly value from your offer?

Create strong competitive advantage for your offer?

Market

For each product or client type, how well do you:

Define your market. The one you are really in?

Know your audience and what they want, their problems/needs/pains/desires?

Know what are they willing to pay to have these solved?

Know what defines this person/their profile compared to everybody else?

Know where you would find them?

Know who the decision makers are and who influences them?

Know who is best placed to introduce your ideal customer to you (your referral sources)?

Know your competitors and how you differentiate
 yourself from them?

Gather the personalised data you need, i.e. names,
 contact details etc?

Organise these contact details using a CRM system or database?

Maintain relationships with customers that buy from you
 or refer you?

Message

For each product or client type, how well do you:

Understand and communicate in your customers' language:

 Clear, benefit-led, concise sales messages?

 Your customers' greatest pain and the problem(s) you
  will solve for them?

 The practical features, how it works, they want most?

 The benefits/unique selling points, the results they want most?

 The emotional benefits that they want most?

 Messages for each part of your customer's sales journey;
  from unaware to ready to buy?

Nurture and develop relationships until they are ready to buy?

Engage your audience (use customer engagement) and not
 just talk about you?

Offer proof that your solutions work, testimonials, case studies,
video demonstrations, free trials, guarantees etc?

Use brand/product endorsements by people
 known/liked/trusted by your audience?

Tell them how to take the next action, ideally right now?

Media

For each product or client category, how well do you:

Select marketing methods according to cost/your budget?

Reach your intended target audience with your
  selected channels?

Illicit a response from your audience with your
  selected channels?

Keep messages consistent across all your media?

Try/test some of the most popular marketing channels such as:

  Networking?

  Website and SEO?

  Email marketing?

  Social media?

  Joint ventures: shared activity/costs, non-competing
  offer to same audience?

Evaluate all possible marketing channels?

Executing the marketing plan

How well do you:

Create a clear plan that focuses your activities for the year?

Match your plan to your marketing budget?

Ensure you have the resources to deliver the plan,
  in-house or outsourced?

Ensure you follow your plan?

Measuring the marketing results

How well do you:

Quantify your marketing ROI (return on investment)?

Make marketing decisions based on facts/data/evidence?

Consistently measure your marketing results/response
rate for each activity?

Measure your marketing effectiveness at each point in
the sales journey?

Test/split test marketing initiatives on a small scale first
(testing/prototyping)?

Ask/record how people found out about you
and/or buy from you?

Analyse results and look for ways to improve on them?

Keep on analysing, testing and improving?

Sales

Of all the areas that make a jet engine work, the point at which compressed air and fuel combust is critical. Without this, there would be no expansion of gases, no turning of turbines, no thrust or lift, and no flight. So it is with a business. Without sales, a business has no power, and will fail to perform. Like the pressured environment in a jet engine, sales and selling can cause the most conflicted feelings compared to all the other areas of a business.

Some people love selling, others hate it. The word is often associated with the pushy salesman who does not listen or does not care, applies too much pressure to the customer, and will do or say anything to get the sale. Good sales people know that selling is about solving the genuine problems, needs, wants, desires of their customers. Needs may be physical, rational or emotional. Selling is about offering appropriate and wanted solutions to fulfil those needs.

Understanding those needs can be an essential part of the sales process. This can be an open conversation with your customer, asking them questions to help them describe in their own words, the wishes they want fulfilled and finding a match, if appropriate, between what they want and the solutions you provide. The better this is done, the easier and less pressured a sale will be, and the more delighted a customer will be with the end result. This approach is called *consultative selling*.

As already discussed in the marketing section, marketing is all activity that attracts and keeps you at the forefront of a customer or potential customer's mind until they are ready to make an enquiry. Sales is all the activity you employ once an enquiry has been made. The two functions overlap, and a good sales process should integrate with marketing activities, especially in three key areas:

1   Messaging aligned with your marketing activities
2   Highlighting your competitive advantage. Why you above all others?
3   The customer sales journey and 5 to 21 touches to a sale

You need to ensure your sales and marketing describes the challenges/ problems/needs/desires of your clients in a similar way, using *their* language. And both marketing and sales activities create touches that help nurture a potential customer until they are ready to commit to working with you.

Repeatable sales processes

Like any good system (see Operations in Chapter 7), a good sales process should be process and information driven, making it:

- Measurable – so you know what works and what to improve
- Repeatable – so your successes or mistakes can be duplicated or eliminated

This may include the following stages:

1 Prospecting: finding new potential clients
2 First contact: finding a way to initiate first contact
3 Qualification: checking for current and future needs to ensure they are relevant to your business
4 Nurturing: maintaining and developing contact with a potential client until their need matures
5 Presentation: explaining the value, benefits, features of your solutions
6 Objection Handling: unpacking emotional and rational blocks to proceeding
7 Closing: asking the client if they would like to commit to the sale
8 Getting referrals: asking for other contacts who may also appreciate your solution

Managed, measured, monitored and improved

As with all parts of The Business Jet Engine®, this process needs to have someone to manage measure and monitor these activities and look for areas of improvement, with agreed timescales for review. To make this effective, you may want to refine your:

- Job descriptions for your salespeople. Ensure all core activities are included
- Training processes. Ensure all sales activities and procedures are consistent
- Sales information system/automation. Ensure all activity is simplified and tracked/recorded
- Sales compensation plan, if used. Ensure it is realistic and motivating

Information = the sales pipeline

To predict your cash flow, and to meet future sales, you need to be measuring the key activities that lead to actual sales. These figures should be based on past performance. If you do not know them, make estimates, and refine them making them more accurate over time based on actual performance. Here is an example:

In one month, you have 200 carefully targeted people you cold-call. These are sometimes called your suspects. Of those suspects, 40% agree to join your email list to stay informed about your products and services, giving you 80 prospects. Of your 80 prospects, 10% reply to an email, requesting more information about an offer, giving you eight enquiries. Of your eight enquiries, 50% make a purchase, giving you four sales. If each sale is worth £500, then your revenue from that activity is £2k per month.

This can be expressed by the following:

200 suspects x 40% = 80 prospects
80 prospects x 10% = 8 enquiries
8 enquiries x 50% = 4 sales
4 x £500 = £2k per month

Giving the ratios:

200:80:8:4 = £2k pm

or

$$100:40:4:2 = £1k\ pm$$

From the ratios, you know that for every:

100 cold calls, you could make £1k pm
200 cold calls, you could make £2k pm

Therefore, if you need to make £4k per month, you would need to make 400 cold calls, assuming the subsequent conversion ratios remain the same. Your annual revenue from this activity would be £48k.

$$£4k\ x\ 12\ months = £48k\ pa$$

Equally, you could look at how to improve your conversion ratios at each stage, so that each part of the sales process is more effective. This could be by increasing the number of suspects you approach, improving your conversion of prospects to enquiries or actual sales. You could also explore how to increase the value of each sale with higher priced or add-on products, and how frequently that customer might buy from you again.

If you measure the average timeframes for each stage
of the sales process, you can use those measures
to predict future sales through regular pipeline
updates and monitoring.

There are many variations and refinements to this example formula. If you have not done it before, start by finding a system that most closely fits with your business, keep it simple and improve it as you go.

Sales Diagnostic Questions

How well do you:

Client Focused

Get customers to tell you what they value, in their own words?

Listen to their needs?

Talk in their language?

Really listen and understand their objectives before
trying to sell?

Ensure you have competitive advantage to deliver
the value they want?

Staff

Recruit competent sales staff?

Ensure the quality of training you provide to your sales force?

Manage your sales staff and processes?

Ensure staff understand your brand values, competitive
advantage & service expectations?

Process & Information

Organise your sales process so it is clear and efficient?

Ensure everyone works to the same approach?
Documented if necessary?

Prioritise the activities that make the biggest difference?

Compare your process with a top performing sales
person or organisation?

Ensure your sales process follows/aligns with your
customer's sales journey?

Information

Ensure you have clear sales objectives and targets,
linked to financial plans?

Measure conversion rates at all stages of your pipeline?

Ensure you have accurate sales forecast/pipeline
information?

Follow-up enquiries or proposals?

Look to analyse and constantly improve
your performance?

Happy Customers

Returning to your jet engine, the cold air that was sucked-in and combusted, is kicked out the back of the engine as hot air. This leaves white trails of condensation. These contrails can linger for minutes or even hours across the sky depending on the atmosphere at that time.

In business, when your clients talk about you, like contrails they leave a highly visible sign of whether or not you delighted or failed their expectations. And their opinion can linger in the minds of others for quite some time. Some businesses may not care, such as monopolies where customers have no choice, or cowboys with no desire for repeat business. But for the rest of us, customer delight is essential.

Given a choice, how often do you return to a business that ripped you off or let you down? For any business wanting a sustainable, long-term future, it has to be a top priority to create happy, delighted customers that say great things about you. These customers will use you again and again, and recommend you to others.

For this, you need to know exactly what your customers think of you. Even if you have delivered everything to your highest possible standards, if the client feels differently, that is their experience. To be certain of this you need to gain customer feedback, which is covered in the next topic. In the meantime, use the diagnostic questions to score how well you create happy customers.

Happy Customers Diagnostic Questions

How would your customers rate:

Your product or end solutions?

Your customer service, how cared about they feel?

Their overall happiness and likelihood of using you again?

Their likelihood of recommending you to friends
   and contacts?

How well do you know:

What they value from you most and why they
   decided to use you?

What they believe you do better than anyone else
   in the same market?

What they score you out of 10, and what is needed
   to score you 10?

What they would most like you to improve, add or change?

How well do you:

Have plans in place to make your score a 10 in the future?

Let your customers know you intend to address this?

Customer Feedback

Hot air and vapour from the jet engine is eventually recycled and reabsorbed back into the atmosphere. In a similar way, customer feedback should be gained and recycled back into your business as market intelligence.

Why gain customer feedback?

'What is value to the customer?'
It may be the most important question,
yet it is the one least often asked. – Peter Drucker

Knowing what your customers value and what they think of you is of central importance. In particular it will help you to:

- Ensure you retain your hard-won customers
- Improve or develop your product or service, now or in the future
- Improve or develop your customer service and experience, now or in the future
- Repair mistakes and avoid critical errors
- Minimise or positively transform bad press/brand reputation
- Gain valuable testimonials and referrals
- Refine your marketing messages

Most businesses cannot answer the question, 'What is value to the customer?' If they do, it is their own opinion, not that of the customer. Knowing precisely what your customers *really* value is inextricably linked to your business success. You need to create raving fans who love what you do, talk about you, recommend you to others, and will return to you for more. This gives any business the strongest foundation.

Methods of gaining customer feedback

These include:

- Asking your client face-to-face
- Feedback forms given to clients or available on site
- Email questionnaires
- Text and messenger platforms
- Website activity
- Press reviews
- Review sites, social media and community sites
- Online surveys such as Survey Monkey
- Feedback review meetings with your clients
- Agencies specialising in research such as:
  - Forums/focus groups
  - Mystery shopper services

When asking for feedback, bear in mind that your customers may not always tell you what they really feel. They may value their relationship with you, and not want to upset you. They may simply wish to avoid a conflict if they believe their negative comments will not be well received.

Enabling customers to give feedback anonymously can help them be more open and honest. An independent researcher can also help customers feel confident that negative comments can be fed back to you, without reference to their source. When possible, and with your clients' permission, in-depth conversations can be summarised to produce testimonials and case studies.

The key to the process is to define what specific feedback you are looking for and why, before deciding how to try and acquire it. What are you most specifically trying to achieve and what is the simplest method to get there?

KISS – keep it short & simple

The longer the process, the more unlikely it is that your customers reach completion. Here are some pointers to avoid this:

- Be respectful of your customer's time
- Be simple, brief and clear where possible
- Ask one question at a time
- Use a consistent rating scale across all questions, where appropriate
- Use open-ended questions where possible

Open-ended questions allow customers to offer their own views and opinions in ways you may not have thought of and avoid questions that are clearly trying to lead the customer to give a specific answer.

You may need to offer customers a bonus to take part. This may be as simple as having their views heard or having a service improved for their benefit, but research shows that a gift of some kind can improve response rates by up to 20%.

Using feedback to improve your business

An obvious benefit of gaining feedback is that you can use it to improve your product or service. For this to take place, you need to know what your customers value, but also what they wish you would provide in addition.

Simple questions to ask

A simple way of doing this is using a technique used throughout this book.
Ask:

> *'How well are we doing out of 10?'*
> *'What makes it a 7?'* (if for example the answer was 7/10)

And then ask:

> *'What's the missing 3 that would make it a 10?'*

Often, this last answer is the most valuable, as it highlights where you most need to improve. To generate ideas for your products or services in the future you could ask:

> *'What could we offer you next year*
> *that would seriously impress you?'*

Using feedback to improve your marketing messaging

By hearing what your customers value from you, in their own words, you can use any frequently used words and phrases to improve your marketing. Marketing messages are better understood when using your clients' language. The feedback process should give you good examples of this.

You may be promoting benefits and features that aren't what your customers really value most. You may be promoting your cafe on having the best tasting coffee, whereas what your customers really like is the friendly service, being known by name, and an atmosphere where customers all talk to each other.

Customer Feedback Diagnostic Questions

How well do you:

Pro-actively ask for and collect customer feedback?

Know what your customers really value most?

Know what they wish you would offer or improve?

Know if they will use you again?

Know if they would recommend you to a friend,
   relative or contact?

Remain receptive to both negative and good feedback?

Use independent research in addition to your own?

Collate and analyse your results?

Monitor your brand reputation everywhere?

How well do you use your customer feedback to:

Improve or develop your product or customer
   service experience?

Repair mistakes and avoid critical errors?

Gain valuable testimonials and referrals?

Improve your marketing message using your
   customers words and phrases?

Marketing to Existing Customers

In some engines, a super-charger uses the already spinning parts of an engine to suck and compress air at a greater rate than would normally be possible, to maximise the air entering the engine, creating an even greater rate of combustion, and hence power from the engine. In our jet engine metaphor, we can use the principle of existing customers in the same way. Why waste all the energy used in gaining and servicing a new customer, only to let them disappear into the atmosphere? Instead, harness all that existing energy for further use.

In business, this is the process of ensuring you give maximum attention to your already hard won customers. In fact, many top marketeers believe that at least 60% of your marketing activities should be directed back to your existing customers. After all, it has taken a lot of time, money and energy for you to create that first sale.

In the first instance, having demonstrated the value that you provide, what else can you offer that they would appreciate? Do they need the same product and service from you again: for example, does their car need servicing by you every year? Do you send reminders? Or are there further products or services you can offer them that are a logical next step from the first purchase: having serviced their car, might they want some new tyres, their scuffed wheels refurbished, or even a new car next year? Your customers may be unaware you provide any of these services unless you make it clear.

A classic business mistake is to stay focused on new business. Existing customers are neglected, and gradually drift away.

Re-Marketing Diagnostic Questions

How well do you:

Consider all your repeat, up-sell and cross-sell
opportunities?

Offer a VIP or premium service for your highest
spending clients?

Ensure you spend significant time marketing to
existing customers?

Calculate the lifetime value of your average customer?

Know which of your customer profiles spend most
with you?

Create a plan to maximise your sales with them?

Execute, measure and monitor success
with that plan?

Gather case studies and testimonials from this
client base?

Create referral strategies with existing customers?

Ask them to refer similar customers like them to you?

Evolving a Marketing-Led Future Strategy

Many successful businesses disappear because they do not evolve with the changing trends and developments in their market environment. For example, how many people still travel by horse and cart, use a fax machine, or buy their music on CD? At one time these were thriving industries. Think of the penalty Kodak paid for not appreciating the speed with which people were moving to digital photography from film, which had been the mainstay of their business for decades. Another example is the demise of Blockbuster Videos, with the rise of on-demand movies over the internet away from physical videos in retail outlets.

To avoid this issue in your own business, choose up to three ideal current clients, the type of clients you would love to build your business around in the future. Arrange to take these clients out for a relaxed and extended conversation. These are typically the clients with which you already have a warm and trusting relationship.

The idea is for you to understand where they see themselves in the future, to create an atmosphere for an in-depth and wide ranging discussion about their issues and challenges, hopes and fears, opportunities and threats. Not just currently or this year, but looking further ahead to maybe one, five or ten years from now. Depending on your personal relationship with them, you may also want to ask how they see their personal lives changing alongside this. This may have an important bearing on how else you can evolve.

Future Strategy Diagnostic Questions

How accurately do you know:

What you do for them that they value most?

What you could most improve or do better?

What challenges they wish you were able to solve for them?

What challenges in general they have no idea how to solve?

Where is their business now and what is going well?

What are their major problems and challenges?

Where they see their business in one, five and ten years?

How they see their industry changing?

What they see as their greatest strengths, weaknesses,
opportunities & threats?

How they hope to adapt and change in response?

How they see you having a role in that future?

How you see your role in that future, and how you may
have to evolve?

How this fits with their hopes and dreams for their
personal lives?

CHAPTER NINE

Fueling your Finances
the importance of cash injection

An engine relies on fuel to create combustion. Compared to the vast volumes of air required, the proportions of fuel are comparatively small. Yet despite this disparity, everyone knows that fuel is essential. If you are boarding an aircraft, regardless of the distance you are travelling, you assume that fuel is carefully loaded in sufficient quantity by the crew for you to reach your destination safely. Anything less would be foolhardy as you would risk falling from the sky.

Manage your finances with precision

Yet, if fuel is to aircraft as finance is to enterprise, then many businesses fly in a cavalier way. Many don't know their financial position. The key instruments of finance are ignored. Budgets, targets, profit and loss statements, balance sheets, cashflow forecasts, credit and debt; these are your dials and controls. For a business to fly, with minimised risk, they need to be understood and used appropriately.

Whether you run a lifestyle business or want to make a fortune, one of your primary needs will be to make money: to create profits for yourself, any investors and to provide staff with an income. Correctly managing your finances with precision ensures you achieve this. Yet so many businesses solely rely on hard work and are then surprised when they become unstuck.

Regardless of size, you need to plan, organise, deliver, control, account, audit, report and improve your financial performance. Some of this you may do yourself, some you may outsource. Either way, you need to ensure that sufficient funds are available at every stage, from start-up and growth through to potential sale, in order to meet all your financial obligations and ambitions. With this in mind the summary concepts that follow are vital for every business.

Pricing

For any business, making money starts with products correctly priced to make a profit. This ensures that you start with a sufficient inflow of cash. To do this, there is a blend of two key factors:

1 Knowing the most your market will let you charge
2 Knowing the least you can charge and still make money

We will look at knowing the least you can charge (by knowing your costs) in the management accounts and planning subsection. Here, we want to focus on maximising your prices to generate maximum profit. This requires an excellent understanding of your competitors' pricing, the marketplace and what the market will pay depending on the perceived value of your offer.

For example, think about flying first class rather than economy. First class passengers pay for more than just travelling from A to B. They are paying for a more exclusive experience and expect to arrive more ready and rested than economy passengers at the other end of their journey.

A first class passenger isn't looking for a flight that is cheap. Even though their ticket may seem extravagant to a budget traveller, they want a fair price for what they get.

Value is about perception and getting a comparatively good deal.
It does not mean your product costs the least.

Be aware that some competitors may suppress your marketplace by unknowingly underpricing themselves. They may not accurately know what it costs to make their product: their cost of sales. They may not know the costs of running their business: their fixed costs. They may not appreciate or pay attention to making a profit. And they may have forgotten to allow for VAT and corporation tax payments.

Out of ignorance, they may approach the market with a price that is attractively cheap for customers, but too low for profits. They may gain a large market share in the short term, effectively stealing work from you on price, but they may not survive in the long term. Especially when those large Inland Revenue payments become due.

If this happens, you need to find a way to compete against them until they have to change strategy or go bust. This can be a challenge, especially if you only compete on price, hence the importance of having competitive advantage. This is how you offer something more valuable to your clients than money. Such as better problem solving, a cooler sexier product, amazing customer service or a more stylish and desirable brand.

The greater your competitive advantage and perceived value, the more you can charge. Charging more gives you an excellent starting point to create profit. Especially when linked to your sales, profit and other financial targets, which we discuss later in this chapter.

Improving your inflow of cash

In addition to pricing, other areas which bring money into your business and improve cashflow include:

- Managing debtor days
  - contractually agree in advance your Terms of Business to minimise when payment is due
- Credit control
  - systemise how you promptly chase and collect late payments
- Regular billing
  - agree monthly payments from clients which smooth your cash-flow and minimise bad debt

Sales targets

Even well-established businesses can have inadequately planned sales targets. Too often, company sales targets are large, rounded-up numbers representing the sales revenue that a business dreams it can achieve, with no further breakdown as to how that will happen. The company strategy to deliver these targets is, 'work 30% harder than last year and sales will be 30% larger than last year'.

A common reason these targets remain vague is believing it will be over-complicated to improve on this. Businesses often feel that to go into more detail, they need 100% accurate sales information, and all sorts of facts and figures before they start. But as they do not have this readily available, and creating it may require painstaking work, considered planning gets ignored.

To overcome this obstacle, the solution is to get started using estimated numbers and simplifying the story you are trying to tell. To do this, take a crude selection of your most popular products at your most popular price bands. Even if you sell over one hundred product lines at twenty price points, force yourself to select no more than four or five average price bands that cover your range.

Put the price bands onto a spreadsheet, and approximate the total number of units you believe you currently sell in each price band.

Example sales targets

You may need to adapt this to suit your business model. For example, a consultancy may be better represented showing bandings of types of clients by annual spend. Some clients may spend £500, some £1k, and some £4k per year on average. You are looking for the simplest representation of what you sell, to whom and in what quantity. Resist believing your business has too many variables, which of course it does. There are always common trends.

The first time you do this, restrain from checking your actual figures. Test this method with estimates and gut-feel. Adjust the numbers until you have a simple and plausible reflection of your current business model and sales figures.

For each product band consider where you are now, and where you really want to be:

- Which is most profitable?
- The type of customer you most easily attract for each band?
- Who you prefer working for?
- Who you best serve?
- Where you have greatest competitive advantage?

Example Sales Targets

Av Product Price	units sold per month	per month	per annum
£5	350	£1,750	£21,000
£50	150	£7,500	£90,000
£200	50	£10,000	£120,000
£500	10	£5,000	£60,000
		£24,250	£291,000
		sales revenue pm	sales revenue pa

These factors may not all be in the same band. If that is the case, you may want to reconsider your business model so they better align.

Experiment with your figures to consider your future sales targets. This is the primary purpose in this exercise; to establish a realistic number of units you need to sell, or clients you need to gain, over a given timeframe. And how you best position yourself to improve your sales over time.

There may be a product band that is most obvious to maximise; you know it is most profitable and you are already positioned to serve it well. Or it may become apparent that you need to adapt to serve a more attractive band.

As you clarify your thinking, you can check the accuracy of your estimates against the facts. Compared to collating infinite detailed information at the outset, quick estimates force you to present your business simply. When the time for refinement comes, you can focus on the facts you really need, saving considerable time. As your plan develops, it needs to be linked to your sales pipeline, marketing and overall business strategy.

This simple exercise is the start of having better sales targets which can be measured and monitored, whilst the figures that form your thinking can be refined as you progress.

Pricing Diagnostic Questions

How well do you:

Pricing

Charge the maximum your clients will pay *and* still
  think they get great value?

Split test your pricing to confirm this?

Offer tiered pricing or a VIP package?

Know your competitors' prices and what they really
  offer for the money?

Price to make a profit after all your costs are considered?

Link your pricing to achievable/realistic sales targets?

Improving cash inflow

Have payment terms *agreed* with clients that best serve
  your business?

Invoice promptly?

Systemise regular and effective credit control?

Agree regular billing where possible?

Minimise your debtor days against industry standards
  to maximise cash in your business?

Sales Targets

Create sales targets based on product or client bandings?

Maximise your most profitable bandings?

Link these to your business plan?

Regularly measure and monitor performance?

Ensure sales staff know their impact on profitability
and your business plans?

Profit

Alongside sales, an even more important target is your profit. Considering that profit is central to your survival, it is surprising how many businesses leave profit-making to chance. This is partly because profit can be seen as a by-product of all your activity. It is like the exhaust at the back of your engine. To some people, like exhaust, profit is a dirty word. There is shame attached to being focused on making money. To others, the exhaust from an engine doesn't really matter. They focus on making the engine work as best they can and whatever exhaust is produced is pure chance.

Many business owners run their business in a similar way. They focus on working hard, doing the best job they can, and see what profit is achieved at the end. They feel they have no control over the result, which is true with this mindset.

If this is you, it may help to understand the four essential ways in which profit can be used:

1 Retained in the business to provide working capital and financial security
2 Re-invested in the business providing funds for growth
3 Paid as dividends to shareholders and investors
4 Used to pay off any debt

The second step in changing your mindset, having realised the essential purpose of profit, is to produce well thought through plans and take control by using management accounts, which we will look at next.

Profit Diagnostic Questions

How well do you:

Profit

Realistically plan to make profit?

Understand both gross and net profit?

Identify your key drivers of profit?

Regularly measure and monitor performance against
these drivers?

Regularly review your profit and loss forecasts and reports?

Use of Profits

Retain sufficient profit to survive three to six months
with no income?

Carefully plan your future use of any profit?

Draw compensation that reflects your contribution
to the business?

Create a return greater than you could earn with an alternative:

Lower risk investment?

Lower stress activity?

Management Accounts and Financial Planning

Management accounts are your primary financial indicators and are used to plan your journey, establish your exact position en-route, and course-correct as required. Businesses looking to raise capital from outside will be required to produce management accounts by potential investors. And regardless of whether or not you require outside investment, you should refresh your own plans every year, however simple, to focus on what you wish to achieve and then measure your progress against those plans.

Tax accounts, often prepared by your accountant, are used to minimise your tax liability in relation to the Inland Revenue. These are different to management accounts which you use to run your business.

Key management accounts

For planning, you need to establish your sales targets, budget and profit forecasts. These will be linked in with the three cornerstones of management accounting:

- Profit & loss – the money you earn and spend
- Cashflow – reflects where your working capital is healthy or at risk
- Balance sheet – your overall position of what you own and what you owe

To create your budget and profit forecasts, you need to understand profit and loss. In addition, you need to understand the difference between forecasts and reports:

- Reports – reflect *past* performance – where you have come from
- Forecasts – for estimating and planning your *future* – where you are going

Your management accounts comprise both forecasts and reports for each area. This creates a cycle of learning, enabling you to improve both your estimates and actual performance. At a more advanced level, you may want to identify other key financial indicators that drive your business specifically, such as:

- Profitability/gross profit margin as a percentage of sales
- Profitability by product line

- Labour efficiency
- Revenue growth rate
- Solvency – current ratio
- Gearing – debt to equity ratio
- Work-in progress – WIP turnover
- Debtor days
- Costs as a % of revenue – payroll, advertising & marketing
- Costs per employee – rent, stationery, travel, phone etc.
- Accounts payable turnover

Note: I have used the commonly known terms of *profit and loss* and *balance sheet* throughout this book. It is more technically correct to refer to profit and loss as an *income statement* and a balance sheet as the *statement of financial position*.

Profit and loss

Working towards your budget and profit forecasts, it is often easiest to start with a monthly profit and loss, which comprises estimates of your:

- Sales targets – what you hope you will sell
- Costs targets – what you hope is the maximum you will spend

Within your costs, there are two main categories:

1 Cost of sales – your costs linked directly to delivering your product or service
2 Fixed costs – what your business costs to run regardless of any sales

Cost of sales – also called direct costs or cost of goods sold

This is what it costs you to make your product or deliver your service. These costs typically vary in that they go up or down more or less in pro-portion to your rise and fall in sales. This can help you identify what is in this category. For example, if you make cakes, the cost of ingredients will increase significantly if you go from making 100 cakes a day to 1,000.

Fixed costs – also called overheads

These are the costs of running your business that stay the same regard-less of how much you sell; for example, your premises, the equipment you use and the salary for your baker who needs to be there whether you make 100 or 1,000 cakes.

If you increase to making 10,000 cakes a day you may need a bigger premises and three bakers. Your fixed costs will increase, but they change only when there is a major fluctuation in quantities, less so with minor changes. Admittedly, this can be a grey area. If you are a design agency and hire freelancers by the project, this cost will vary as you win more projects, and may go in cost of sales.

Gross and net profit

There are two main profit targets you need to calculate using both cost of sales and fixed costs: gross profit and net profit:

Gross Profit = Sales Revenue – Cost of Sales

Net Profit = Sales Revenue – Cost of Sales – Fixed Costs

For example:

£4k Sales Revenue – **£2k** Cost of Sales = **£2k** Gross Profit

£4k Sales Revenue – **£2k** Cost of Sales – **£1k** Fixed Costs **= £1k Net Profit**

These figures can be built into a spreadsheet to give you a monthly or annual profit & loss statement.

Example profit and loss for one month

This example (on page 172) is for an event company for one month. Although the events themselves appear to make £2k gross profit, when all other costs are factored in, the business shows a net loss, rather than profit, of £1k. Based on January alone, this isn't a viable business.

These estimates can then form the foundations of an annual budget which we will look at next.

Example Profit & Loss

	January
Sales Revenue	**£4,000**
Cost of Sale	
Venue	£1,000
Event Staff	£500
Food	£300
Insurance/Other	£200
Cost of Sales	**£2,000**
Gross Profit	**£2,000**
Fixed Costs	
Office	£800
Salaries	£1,400
Sales&Marketing	£500
Computing	£100
Professional	£80
Transport	£40
Insurance etc	£30
Sundries	£50
Fixed Costs Total	**£3,000**
Net Profit	**-£1,000**

Budgets and cashflow
Budgeting

When your monthly figures, both sales and costs, are estimated for 12 months ahead, this creates an annual budget which can be used as a target to ensure you make a profit.

Example 12 month budget forecast

Continuing the example of our events company, to become more viable they plan to run additional events in the spring and autumn as these are peak seasons. By increasing sales significantly in those months, with their fixed costs staying the same throughout the year, their annual gross profit is now £49,800.

When their fixed costs are factored in, the business shows an annual net profit of £13,800, which will then attract corporation tax. The business owners need to decide if this is a worthwhile level of profit for the effort required. If not, they need to decide which figures to try and increase such as sales revenue or reduce such as venue or staff costs, until the net profit becomes rewarding.

Example Budget Forecast

	Jan	Feb	Mar	Apr	May	Jun	Jul	Aug	Sep	Oct	Nov	Dec	Total
Sales Revenue	0	4,000	8,000	16,000	8,000	4,000	4,000	4,000	8,000	16,000	8,000	4,000	84,000
Cost of Sale													
Venue	0	800	1,600	2,400	1,600	800	800	800	1,600	2,400	1,600	800	15,200
Event Staff	0	500	1,000	1,500	1,000	500	500	500	1,000	1,500	1,000	500	9,500
Food	0	300	600	900	600	300	300	300	600	900	600	300	5,700
Insurance/Other	0	200	400	600	400	200	200	200	400	600	400	200	3,800
Cost of Sales Total	0	1,800	3,600	5,400	3,600	1,800	1,800	1,800	3,600	5,400	3,600	1,800	34,200
Gross Profit	0	2,200	4,400	10,600	4,400	2,200	2,200	2,200	4,400	10,600	4,400	2,200	49,800
Fixed Costs													
Office	800	800	800	800	800	800	800	800	800	800	800	800	9,600
Salaries	1,400	1,400	1,400	1,400	1,400	1,400	1,400	1,400	1,400	1,400	1,400	1,400	16,800
Sales&Marketing	500	500	500	500	500	500	500	500	500	500	500	500	6,000
Computing	100	100	100	100	100	100	100	100	100	100	100	100	1,200
Professional Services	80	80	80	80	80	80	80	80	80	80	80	80	960
Transport	40	40	40	40	40	40	40	40	40	40	40	40	480
Insurance etc	30	30	30	30	30	30	30	30	30	30	30	30	360
Sundries	50	50	50	50	50	50	50	50	50	50	50	50	600
Fixed Costs Total	3,000	3,000	3,000	3,000	3,000	3,000	3,000	3,000	3,000	3,000	3,000	3,000	36,000
Net Profit	-3,000	-800	1,400	7,600	1,400	-800	-800	-800	1,400	7,600	1,400	-800	13,800
Starting Balance	2,000	-1,000	-1,800	-400	7,200	8,600	7,800	7,000	6,200	7,600	15,200	16,600	
Closing Balance	-1,000	-1,800	-400	7,200	8,600	7,800	7,000	6,200	7,600	15,200	16,600	15,800	

Note that a budget is shown net of VAT (without VAT). In this example, an approximate bank balance has been added in the bottom two rows to crudely show where cashflow may be at risk.

Cashflow and balance sheets

Cashflow shows the exact amounts of cash going through your business at any given time. It differs from a budget in that it is gross of VAT (includes VAT), and perhaps more importantly, reflects when cash is paid out or received in. This is important, because your budget may simplify these facts and show everything for one job happening in the same month.

For example, for one project, a manufacturer, may have materials to pay for in advance, ongoing factory and staff costs, and the cost of delivery. To offset this, they may request their client make part-payments; in advance, for work in progress, and on receipt of goods (or even up to 90 days after delivery). So for one project, related cash going in or out of their business could be spread over many months, and have unexpected impacts on their bank balance.

Although your budget can be developed into a spreadsheet to show cashflow, this is a more complex exercise. Modern accounting software makes this an easier task, so may be an option. Also be aware that there is cash accounting and accrual accounting. However, these concepts are beyond the scope of this book, and best discussed with your bookkeeper or accountant to find the approach best suited to you.

In addition, your balance sheet shows your overall financial position. Even if the timing of your payments and receipts become confusing or hard to ensure, your balance sheet (or statement of financial position) gives you a snapshot of exactly what you owe and are owed. Your cashflow statements work alongside your balance sheet to ensure you have working cash in your bank account as you need it.

Controlling costs

To generate profit, you need to do more than drive sales – you need to manage and minimise your costs to ensure they are within budget.

> *It is a common failing to maximise sales, but to find at year end, that all profit has been nullified by excess spending.*

To avoid this, create your spending budget and stick to it. This includes:
- Controlling impulse buys by sticking to your budget
- Ensuring staff spending is appropriate and necessary via clear lines of authority
- Review supplier contracts for value including leases, utilities and insurance
- Stock control to ensure availability whilst avoiding write-offs or cash tied-up

Management Accounts Diagnostic Questions

How well do you:

Management Accounts

Know the difference between management accounts,
tax accounts and investor accounts?

Produce timely management accounts best suited
to your business?

Measure and monitor financial performance in general?

Use management accounts to make informed decisions?

Produce annual forecasts and reports, updated monthly/regularly for:

Sales/revenue targets?

Budget/profit & loss?

Balance sheet?

Cashflow?

Other key financial business drivers?

Specific Financial KPIs

Identify your most significant costs to monitor closely?

Calculate ROI (return on investment) on costs that
drive performance?

Identify other financial KPIs that show the performance
of your business?

Cashflow and Working Capital

Ensure the business has a strong credit rating?

Ensure all payables are up-to-date?

Track actual cashflow against projections?

Have a good dividend flow to the owners provided by cashflow?

Keep inventory turnover below industry average?

Keep funding of capital expenditure timed to match
the life of the asset?

Ensure current assets exceed current liabilities, after
adjustment for illiquid items?

Control of Costs

Control impulse buys by sticking to your budget?

Ensure clear lines of authority and limits on staff spending?

Review supplier contracts for value, including leases,
utilities and insurance?

Control stock to ensure availability whilst avoiding
write-offs or cash tied-up?

Investing, Re-Investing, Funding and Raising Finance

This activity is about anticipating the future needs of the business, at different stages of growth, and finding the most cost effective route to putting that funding in place. This helps you to ensure that you have all the resources you need to achieve your plans. There is clearly a balance between what you invest in your growth, therefore spending your profit, and retaining profit in the business for security, or to pay shareholders and investors.

To be best placed to deliver your business strategy, you want to be as up-to-date as possible with people, technology and infrastructure. It is clearly a balancing act between the money you spend to grow, and the profit you need/want to make. Growth nearly always has a short to medium-term impact by reducing your profit.

If you are not generating sufficient profit to grow at the rate at which you would like through organic growth, you may wish to consider outside investment, which might include:

- Banks and financial institutions
- Business angels
- Crowd funding
- Funding circle
- Family and friends
- Staff

Alongside banks, specialist organisations and individuals exist who can advise and guide you through the myriad range of options most suited to your needs. These specialists can be especially useful in finding alternatives to a standard bank loan, especially where tax relief, grants or funding may exist.

Investment and Re-investment Diagnostic Questions

How well do you:

For current activities

Ensure you are up to date with all key resources?

Ensure adequate shareholder funds on the balance sheet
for current activities?

Balance retained cash for security whilst investing in
necessary improvements?

For future growth

Fund growth organically?

Know levels of funding available from shareholders
(or others) for growth?

Know what additional options are available when
financing growth?

Know what lenders will look for if you wish to apply
for funding?

Know if you are getting a good deal on finance?

Other Key Concepts of Good Financial Management

These include:

- Capital Structure
  - how you exist as a legal entity, such as sole trader, limited company etc.
- Bookkeeping & Accounting Methods
  - how you record and manage your finances, and remain compliant with HMRC
- Employing Staff
  - dealing with PAYE, national insurance, pensions/auto-enrolment etc.
- Tax
  - how you plan for, minimise and save for any necessary tax payments

These however, are beyond the scope of this book. If you are unsure of these areas then talk to your accountant and/or bookkeeper who should be able to advise you. If you don't have one, then it may be worth an initial consultation to find out how they can help. As always, when looking to hire any resource, have meetings with at least three candidates to assess the best fit for you.

In summary, all the financial elements of your business are focused on one thing: surviving and thriving so you reach the future you desire. Cash is the fuel in your engine. If the flow stops, your business crashes and may not survive. The ideal is to have a surplus of cash that allows your business to grow as you would wish. This will only occur with the necessary planning, measurements, analysis and improvements.

General Finance Diagnostic Questions

How well do you:

Use the trading entity/best structure for you now
and moving forward?

Explore restructuring your business to maximise tax savings?

Ensure you get best advice to minimise your tax liability?

Plan and separate money for taxes and VAT?

Pay taxes and VAT on time?

Deal with financial issues as they arise?

Accounting and Bookkeeping

Ensure you use accounting methods or software best
suited to your needs?

Manage your financial systems and processes?

Get timely information without overload?

Have regular contact with your advisors?

Ultimately, know how your business is running?

Business Value and Sale

Plan for an exit/end-goal/sale?

Ensure your business looks attractive to an external
buyer, today?

Demonstrate growth over the last three years in:

Profitability?

The value of your business?

CHAPTER TEN

Lift-Off with People

perfecting the profile of your wing

The greatest breakthrough in the history of flight came on December 17, 1903 with the Wright brothers when they made the first controlled, sustained flight of a powered aircraft that was heavier-than-air. They achieved this, not through the development of powerful engines, which was the focus of their peers, but by mastering wing and tail profiles and the mechanics for subtle in-flight adjustments.

They understood, that regardless of engine power, their flight would be unstable if they had no control of their wing. It also needed to be correctly profiled for their craft. That concept continues in aircraft today. There are thousands of wing designs, which need to be perfectly suited to their use.

Similarly, your people are like your wing. They need to have the right profile, perfectly suited to you and your business. And as the pilot of your business, you need to understand the mechanics of leadership that allow you to create lift and direction, so your business goes where you would like it to go. If you get these fundamentals right, your plane will be a comparative dream to fly. If you proceed in ignorance, your flight will be unstable and you will struggle to keep control.

People are the most critical part of your business

Regardless of the technology or automation involved, your business ultimately relies on human effort to succeed. Whatever your product or service, there is a human at either end of the chain. It is human input that controls the system at the start, and a human that eventually receives the output at the end. It is the human element that creates the defining difference.

However, people are the most unpredictable part of any system. You may think you know someone well, but they will still have capacity to surprise you. People are made up of mind, body, spirit and emotion. They contain a legacy of biological DNA and cultural conditioning, a cocktail of rational and irrational thought, fuelled by hormones and bio-chemical reactions which can be activated positively or negatively by a spectrum of triggers.

People are the most complex and unpredictable part of any system.

Though unpredictable, people are also the most essential. They are the only part of your business with a genuine ability to understand, empathise, motivate, innovate and communicate. Ask the leader of any large organisation, "What is your greatest challenge?" and most often it will be their personnel. Getting the people-part of a business right requires more care than most leaders are prepared to give. But if you master it, the rewards will be significant.

The Importance of Quality Staff

If you want to have the right profile wing on your Business Jet Engine®, you need to assess the quality of your staff. Poor staff will create 80% of your problems and take 80% of your time. They will underperform and create additional issues. You risk spending too much time trying to get them to a standard they may never reach.

By contrast, staff well suited to their role, with the appropriate attitude and training, will remove 80% of your challenges. You will spend profitable time with them planning and liaising. They will take your problems away and bring them back solved, freeing you to manage your business instead of underperforming team members.

Staff grading

To do this, you need a simple grading system where staff can be scored in three key areas of performance:

1 **Competence** – the job they are paid to do
2 **Drive & motivation** – their commitment to your business succeeding
3 **Relationships** – how well they work with everyone

Where:

    10 = exceptional
    5 = just adequate
    0 = exceptionally poor

Score your staff for each area, then create an overall average score where:

    A-players = 8–10
    B-players = 7–8
    C-players = 5–7
    D-players = 3–5

Note: Staff scored on the boundaries are reflected as such, i.e: 5 = C/D, 7 = B/C and 8 = A/B.

Many businesses fall into the trap of only grading staff against their competence. This accounts for only a third of their contribution. Attitude, drive, motivation, teamwork, inter-personal and relational skills are of equal importance, reflecting the greater part of their performance in your business.

In simple terms, A and B players are your top staff. You want to build your future with these. C players, though useful, represent the industry average, so offer you little in terms of competitive edge. D players are below average and will generally drain your resources unless you can train, develop and re-energise them.

Having established the quality of your staff, you need to look at your human resource and leadership processes. These are how you attract, develop and keep the best people, and also work with those who are underperforming.

Quality Staff Diagnostic Questions

Overall, how well do your staff:

Competence

Demonstrate competence at what they are paid to do?

Prioritise and complete projects on time?

Complete projects to the required standard?

Enhance the company culture?

Remain alert to opportunities and threats?

Solve problems alone and in a team?

Adapt to and work with change?

Drive & motivation

Demonstrate personal drive to succeed in their role?

Demonstrate drive and motivation for your
    business to succeed?

Go the extra mile?

Do whatever it takes?

Always look to improve themselves and the business?

Managing relationships

How well do your staff remain energised and work well with:

Customers?

Their own team?

Suppliers?

You and the company leadership?

How well do they:

Look forward to working together?

Like and respect each other professionally?

Like and respect each other personally?

Trust each other, professionally and personally?

Staff

How well do you:

Ensure you have the best staff?

Regularly review the quality of your staff?

Make staff a top priority?

Use a comprehensive grading system?

Discuss your grading system with your staff?

Use that grading system for motivation and development?

Human Resources and Leadership Processes

Since the 1970s there has been a radical shift in styles of leadership and management in business. Before that, the more traditional style of leadership prevailed, one person dictating and micromanaging from the top, exerting command and control. However, with the introduction of computers and technology, change started to happen too quickly for that style to remain effective.

The world was becoming too complex for the majority of decisions to be filtered down through a chain of command. The faster the change, the faster the response required. Decision-making had to be made by those with the problem in front of their eyes, those best placed to see what was needed that instant.

The modern style of leadership

For progressive organisations, a new form of leadership and management became increasingly successful. Phrases such as 'engaging hearts and minds' became the norm as people were increasingly valued and required to solve problems at every level of business. This is how we reach the point we are at today. The most successful companies recognise the importance of engaging the problem-solving ability of every person in a business and aligning that energy and talent with the company mission and objectives. Where this does not happen, that business will fall behind.

The following are key processes that should be driven by human resources and the leadership teams of a business. Being able to tap into the physical, emotional and intellectual ability of every employee has become central to business success, which starts with getting the right staff, and how you hire.

Hiring

If having the best staff is a mission-critical activity, then we need to question why many novice and seasoned business leaders fall into the trap of hiring too quickly and firing too slowly. Too many managers hire staff, ill-suited to the required task, then struggle to help them perform.

The focus is to fill a vacancy as fast as possible. 'Get the seat filled' is a common mantra. Yet some experts say that a mis-hire can cost a business up to 20 times that person's salary if you look at the time wasted throughout the whole process, lost business opportunities, damage to the business due to poor performance or loss of credibility with clients/ suppliers etc.

To avoid this pitfall, you need to become expert at hiring. You need to ensure you end up employing candidates with the appropriate values, attitude, skills, problem-solving, communication, teamwork and relation-ship abilities for their intended role. Yet many businesses get impatient and employ in a hurry staff that they later regret, and then have to repeat the process anyway. The opposite approach is to recognise the wisdom of hiring once, but taking time to hire only appropriate candidates who meet your criteria.

Induction

Once hired, best practice is to use a thought-out induction process to introduce new team members to their role and the wider company. This can include key aspects that give the company its edge, such as its vision, mission, values and competitive advantage, as well as operational and staff policies such as job descriptions & contracts, staff handbooks and operations manuals, health and safety and manual handling. Depending on the size of your company, many of these written documents are now considered best practice, if not law.

Delegation and training

If you cannot delegate a task to an employee with confidence, it is a cue that they require training.

You may forget how long it took you to develop your own level of skill. It is easy to expect less experienced employees to take over tasks that, to you, now seem easy and common sense. This results in you becoming increasingly frustrated in other peoples' lack of competence, and increas-ingly reluctant to delegate key tasks. Unless an employee arrives with an existing skill set and proven track record, a structured training path is required. This insight is often ignored with the ensuing frustrations. Training plans ensure an employee can perform to standard, and successfully respond to delegated tasks.

Ongoing development and reviews

In addition to initial training, best practice also suggests regular meetings to review an employee's progress against their tasks and role. If you resort to an annual review your staff may see this solely as a pay-review.

Best practice suggests:

- Monthly one-to-one reviews – for quick updates on progress
- Quarterly appraisals – for a more in-depth discussion of development and training needs
- Annual reviews – to look at an employee's overall career path and salary expectations

This ensures that an employee feels valued and their skills development planned, measured and monitored. Any lapse in performance can be discussed, without making it a major issue. In return, the employee has a regular opportunity to raise concerns about their role or employment. Both parties should feel confident that they have a shared plan and clear agreements to move forward.

Disciplinary procedures

This area is considered by many as the most unpleasant and difficult aspect of leadership, and an area that you may understandably wish to ignore. However, staff allowed to underperform set the standard for everyone in your business. In addition, your ability as a leader and manager is put in doubt when you ignore underperformance and let it continue unchecked. No-one, including the underperforming employee, respects a leader who does this.

It may reach the stage where a member of staff struggles to perform at the required standard. Despite appropriate support and training, they either lack the aptitude or desire to succeed. In this case it is essential for the sake of everyone involved that you address the issue. At this critical time, it is essential to enter a formal process. Seek legal advice to ensure that you follow all processes appropriately. In many ways, it is no kindness to your member of staff to allow them to stay in a job at which they cannot succeed. If all attempts to raise their performance fail, then you need to support them in finding another role within the company where they might excel, or look at other career paths which may suit them better.

Note: Current employment law creates a fine line between what would be decent human behaviour such as helping an individual make a career choice elsewhere for which they have greater aptitude, and what could be seen as *constructive dismissal* for which you as an employer can be penalised. Again, legal advice is essential before embarking on such a route.

Motivation

A motivated team is normally a high performing team. The team leader, formally nominated or otherwise, has a major influence in this area. Even unconscious cues such the leader's true-felt commitment to the goal, their energy levels and mood, get picked up and amplified by the team, like ripples across a pond.

There are many theories of motivation, far too many to cover here. At the heart of all motivation is the need to create a desirable future for every person involved. This is rarely created by just salary, perks, rewards or objectives. It requires a deeper understanding of each team member and what matters to them as a human being, not just in their work and career but also in their personal life. Their work goals need to match their deepest passions.

True motivation occurs when there is a close match between a person's career and what they personally wish to achieve. Ultimately, the best way to establish this is by you or an appropriate manager talking to them and finding out what motivates them and ensuring their work goals support this.

Culture starts at the top

Just as with motivation, one of the simplest lessons of leadership is that a company's culture comes from the top. Whatever you might say, it is what you as a leader believe, feel, think and do that gets picked up and mirrored by all. As with parenting, you have to exhibit and embody the culture that you want.

As a leader, it is not what you <u>say</u>, but what you <u>do</u> that counts.

A summary of leadership

Your role as a leader is to engage your team in the vital tasks that allow your business to survive and thrive. You need to provide direction, create enthusiasm and engagement, helping teams work in a coordinated and appropriate manner. You need to ensure that staff are trained to turn plans into actions. Individuals need to be held to account, progress measured and obstacles and problems solved along the way for timely outcomes. Throughout, all communication and agreements should be appropriate and clear.

This is no small task. A task which many leaders take on without formal training, simply copying the role models from their past, successfully or otherwise. With this in mind, formal leadership training or coaching can pay dividends to develop your own skill in this area.

From our Business Jet Engine® model, perfecting and controlling the wing is the area that took mankind a long time to understand in the bid to master flight. Great leadership is about perfecting the profile of your staff and learning the art of flying your plane, working the fine controls that keep your craft pointing where you most need it to go.

HR and Leadership Process Diagnostic Questions

Hiring, recruitment and induction

How well do you:

Clearly identify all skills and attributes required before
   you advertise?

Test-drive candidates before hiring?

Call references and discuss potential employees in-depth?

Ensure job descriptions, employment contracts,
   staff handbooks etc are in place?

Have an induction and training process in place for new staff?

Use a sufficient probationary period before offering a
   full contract?

Staff motivation, performance, development and retention

How well do you ensure:

Roles and responsibilities are clearly defined and
   understood by all?

Staff know how to succeed in their role?

There is a formal review and appraisal system in place?

Performance metrics are in place to measure success?

Training and ways to improve are regularly discussed?

You have highly motivated staff?

Staff know how their role links to the success of the business?

Staff see a desirable future for their career and personal lives?

Your compensation packages are competitive?

There is a clear career and training path for staff at all levels?

Personnel records are complete and up-to-date?

The appropriate policies are in place, and staff are
aware of them?

There are clear disciplinary and grievance procedures
in place?

You keep up-to-date with changes in employment law
or engage professional advice?

Your staff retention is high?

Leadership

How well do you and your leadership team ensure:

Staff understand the priorities for the business to succeed?

There is a deeper vision and mission that everybody
believes in?

Everybody is working towards the same ultimate goals?

The senior leadership team work effectively together to
steer the company?

Key people know their role in creating a strong culture?

You have agreed problem-solving methods?

Required changes are clearly explained before implementation?

High-risk changes are tested and prototyped before
full implementation?

Key individuals are made accountable for implementing change?

Senior staff receive leadership/management training?

The quality of staff relationships are carefully monitored?

There is a succession plan for key roles?

Communication is appropriate so people are motivated and engaged?

Communication is effective so people are clear what is expected?

People are talked to as human beings, not as robots, idiots or numbers?

Everyone has complete information for mission critical work?

CHAPTER ELEVEN

Running Your Airline
planning and monitoring progress

If you have read every chapter of The Business Jet Engine® so far, you have covered the heart of your jet engine, the hard mechanics as your product, customer service and operations. You have your sales and marketing as air, and your finances as fuel: combined these bring your engine alive and give it thrust. You have the right staff as your perfect profile wings to give you lift for take off. These components are held together by the fuselage, which is your business entity as a whole. But critical to all of this is your cockpit and pilot.

The cockpit is where careful planning and consideration is given to all aspects of your journey, from start to end. The pilot needs the skill to fly, instruments to navigate, and the ability to make adjustments as conditions change. As the pilot and cockpit are essential for a plane: planning and measuring progress are essential for your business.

What is Business Planning?

Business planning is the activity of deciding where your business needs to go for greatest success. The process helps you consider the main factors to achieve your goals, anticipate the potential risks, and changes and obstacles that may prevent you from getting there.

A pilot flying from London to New York will consider all the factors needed to cover that distance safely and successfully: the capabilities of the aircraft, the fuel required, the weight of permissible luggage, flight paths and weather conditions. At HQ, additional concerns include pricing of tickets and the number of customers required to make a profit, competitive airlines, legal and safety compliance, terrorism and war zones etc. These tasks require the expertise of many people to succeed.

If you are new to business and still developing parts of your Business Jet Engine® this may sound daunting. However, do not be discouraged. You can keep your planning short and simple, as would a pilot making a short flight by light aircraft in daylight. Clearly, the further the distance and the more ambitious the journey, the greater the complexity of the planning required. Business planning is the same. The more sophisticated and complex the business, the more detailed the planning.

Simple or complex, having simple, clearly defined goals is paramount, hence the power of The Business Jet Engine®. Having goals in place gives you an immediate start but ultimately, they need to serve your long-term plan. Develop your plans and goals as and when you can, and revisit them at least annually.

The fundamental parts of a business plan

Over time, you should consider the following:

Business Purpose	SWOT analysis
Vision	Strengths – internal
Mission	Weaknesses – internal
Company values	Opportunities – external
Customer values	Threats – external
Competitive advantage & USP	

Business Goals & Objectives
Long term – 10 year/exit plan
Medium term – 3 to 5 year
Short term – 1 year

Departmental Goals & Objectives
Product & Service
Operations
Sales & Marketing
Finance
People

Business Drivers/KPIs

If this sounds like an overwhelming task, let me offer an example; the following plan, which I used for my own business a number of years ago. It was produced in about an hour and gave me a good sense of what to focus on for the year ahead.

Many businesses fail because of poor focus,
not because of lack of effort and hard work.

90% of leadership is about what you say *no* to. The remaining 10% you say *yes* to gives you focus. There are so many possibilities, if you chase every opportunity, you will be overwhelmed and confused.

If you stay focused, as you achieve success, you can develop a more comprehensive plan. In addition, a simple plan gets your team onboard. It is quick to read, easy to understand, and simple to refer back to. A vast plan gets easily forgotten.

You will notice that the second part of the plan, Level Two Planning, is incomplete. Though not ideal, I did have a sense of how I was going to approach those areas. I had simple spreadsheets for sales targets and a rough budget. The other areas I thought about as I went along. I clarified them in my head, but did not write them down until I developed the plan the following year. The plan, however, did give me focus by answering eight core questions:

What – do my customers want and I am good at?

Why – do I want to do this?

How – will I achieve this?

Who – is it aimed at?

Where – will I focus geographically?

When – will I achieve my goals?

How much – activity is required to achieve my financial targets?

At what cost – are my expected earning and expenses?

Example simple business plan

Strategic Plan: April Year XXYY – Year XXZZ

MR-Leadership Development

Level One Planning:
What we do:
Get business leaders working on their business, not in it.
Get leadership teams working together effectively.
Get staff thinking like business owners . . .
. . . through ongoing one-to-one or group coaching/mentoring/development/training.

Key goal: *to be the leadership coach of choice in the 1066 area.*
Success = the first name people suggest when recommending a leadership coach.

Why:
To increase the success of local businesses.
To raise the quality of life in the community, including my own.
To spend my professional time doing what I am most passionate about.

How:
Creating improved awareness of key leadership concepts
 – applied to the client's own business.
Change starts with awareness:
 Exploration of the client's challenges and opportunities.
 Introduction of the most valuable insights of business, management,
  leadership & psychology.
 Help clients create and evaluate options and next steps.
  Create accountability for next actions.
Avoid clichés and mundane ideas.

Who:
Delivered by Martin Riley.
For CEOs, MDs, business owners and their leadership teams.
SME's, typically £ 1- 30M turnover. 5 – 50 staff in the local area.

Where:
Hastings, Battle, Eastbourne triangle (primary focus).
Brighton, Tunbridge Wells, Rye (secondary),
South & East UK (tertiary).

When:
Financial Year April XXYY–XXZZ

How much:
X sessions per month charged out at £X producing £X turnover,
 at £X cost = £X profit.
X number of clients, tier 1. Y number of clients, tier 2.

At what cost:
Requires X new clients per month.
£X and X hours per month on sales and marketing activities.
£X business running costs.

Differentiators/Core Competence:
Core material:
Tried and tested:

> 20+ years evolution of original/proprietary material, developed with top executives: CEOs, MDs, business owners, senior executives at top companies in London and New York.

Walk my Talk:
Only work with material that I use myself, has real benefit in my business
  and personal life.
If I do not believe it, understand it or use it, I do not inflict it on my clients.
Avoid the *industry clichés*: information, jargon, techniques
  with little/no real-world value.

The Design Approach:
Complex ideas made simple and easy to use through better designed systems
  and tools.
Clients applying creative problem solving to their greatest challenges/opportunities.
Do not use generic solutions. Ensure they apply to the client's situation and need.
Solutions must not be applied by or rely on me. I remain a coach, not their
  management team.
MR: 30 years design experience – including top London consultancies.

USP/Tag Line/Catch Phrases
External :
Business leaders working on their business, not just in it.
Leadership teams working together effectively.
Staff thinking like business owners.

Internal:
The Apple Mac of Leadership Development.
Keeping it clear, simple and easy to use. Genuine. Soulful.
  Carefully thought through.
The *Design Approach* as a key ingredient: making the complex simple and relevant.

MR-L's *Values/Four Rules:*
* Concepts must be clear, simple and easy to use.
* Enables the client to transform their world.
* Total respect, always, for the client and for myself.
* Care. From the heart. With passion & soul.

Level Two Planning:
Main Obstacles:

MR-L SWOT:
Strengths (internal):
Weaknesses (internal):
Opportunities (external):
Threats (external):

Competitors SWOT:
Strengths (internal):
Weaknesses (internal):
Opportunities (external):
Threats (external):

PESTEL:
Political:
Economic:
Social:
Technological:
Environmental:
Legal:

Product/Service Development Plan:
Current services:
New services:
Long-term product/service development:

Operational:
Most mission critical/vital processes – what to improve:
Most costly processes (time/money/energy) – what to improve:

Sales & Marketing Plan:
Routes to market (ideally x4):
Customer Relations Management:

Financial Plan:
Cash flow forecasts:
Profit & loss statement:
Balance sheets:

Human Resource Development Plan:
Hiring:
Firing:
Appraisals:
Development & training:

For more developed plans you need to consider:

Vision and mission statements

It can be hard to understand the difference between vision and mission statements. Many explanations are confusing with examples that could fit in either category. Although both statements create a far-off goal that focuses your planning, they are subtly different.

Vision Statements

A vision statement creates the furthest-off point in the reader's mind, and is mostly inspirational rather than specific. It is an idealised future state which your business wants to achieve in the long-term.

Virgin Atlantic
To embrace the human spirit and let fly.

Alzheimer's Association
Our vision is a world without Alzheimer's disease.

Mission Statements

A mission statement, by contrast, is more specific. It is more about the guiding principles, the *what, why and how*. It tends to reflect the current situation and how the vision may be realised in the next one to three years. In effect, the vision may change little over a company's lifetime, but the mission could change more often, as the company adapts to an ever-changing world.

Starbucks
Vision: *To establish Starbucks as the premier purveyor of the finest coffee in the world while maintaining our uncompromising principles while we grow.*
Mission: *To inspire and nurture the human spirit – one person, one cup and one neighbourhood at a time.*

IKEA

Vision: *At IKEA our vision is to create a better everyday life for many people.*
Mission: *Our business idea supports this vision by offering a wide range of well-designed functional home furnishing products at prices so low that as many people as possible will be able to afford them.*

The Business Jet Engine®

Vision: *To raise the success rate and quality of life for SME businesses and owners worldwide.*
Mission: *By providing a simple guide and support tools that make business planning easier and simpler.*

Well considered statements should inspire people. They should create genuine passion and purpose beyond just making money. Working for a living is a need to be fulfilled, a necessary requirement. To create greater drive and passion, people require purpose and meaning beyond creating company profits. They need a meaningful, worthwhile end goal.

Company values

This links together a host of concepts such as beliefs, values, rules and norms. The purpose of this area is for you to consider how you are perceived, internally and externally. What are seen as your qualities, character, standards and behaviour? How do you want to be known and seen by your customers, suppliers, competitors. And above all, how do you want your own staff to feel, as they have to embody the qualities you wish to convey?

In brief, the key areas can be thought of as:

- Beliefs
  - How you think your world works. The stories you tell to make sense of it.
- Values
  - What you think is good, bad, right or wrong.
  - The things of which you approve and disapprove; want more or less of.

- Rules and Norms
    - The way you and your people behave.
    - The behaviour you reward or punish, encourage or discourage, exhibit or hide.

Customer values

Just as you need to consider your own beliefs and values, you need to consider those of your customers. What do they care about, most need and want, think is good, bad, right or wrong? You need to repeat the same values questions from their perspective. Rather than guess, you need to ask them and listen carefully to their answers. Ensure you have understood them by explaining it back to them in *their* language, not *yours*.

Above all, watch their behaviour to ensure it matches their claims. Any gap between their declared values and actual behaviour may be a clue to what they really value, and want you to provide.

Do you know anybody that espouses honesty, but cannot refrain from white lies? For them, avoiding conflict may override the desire for total transparency. Watch for actions as well as words. Despite what they say, what do they really want from you?

This level of client understanding may seem over-involved for your average small business. But by deeply understanding your clients' needs, you will be better placed to fulfil them. You do not need to do everything at once, but aim for this clarity over time. Which leads us to competitive advantage, the heart of our next planning concept.

Competitive advantage – including USPs, differentiation and core competence

We need to build upon the concept of competitive advantage from Chapter 7. Simply, if you do not have it, you may as well not compete. Without it, you will always be struggling to stand out from the competition. If you find a brand new market without any competition, if you start to make money, competition will be sure to follow.

The simplest way to understand competitive advantage is to imagine two circles.

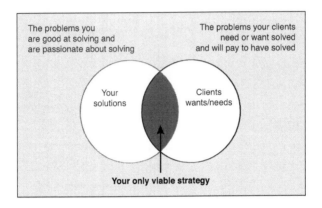

The problems you are good at solving and are passionate about solving

The problems your clients need or want solved and will pay to have solved

Your solutions

Clients wants/needs

Your only viable strategy

The circle on the left represents the problems you love to solve, are good at solving, are passionate about solving, and are hopefully better at solving than anyone else. Too many businesses set out to make their fortune from this circle alone. It is important you do something you love. But on its own, it is not enough without a market for what you do.

For example, a small shop opened in town selling wooden sculptures from Africa. It looked like the owners loved to travel and had found items they could buy cheaply, and return home to sell. However, in this town with conservative tastes, few people were passionate about buying these sculptures for their homes. It was no surprise that within a few months the store had closed.

The circle on the right are the problems your clients need, want, would love to have and will pay to have solved. You need to be confident that they don't just say they want your solution, but they will actually part with their money.

If you focus solely on the right hand circle and enter a market for purely mercenary reasons but have no skill or passion for what you do, you run the risk of being seen as cynical. This is the terrain of cowboys and uncaring monopolies. You cannot build a positive reputation from here. When people have choice, they will move to a supplier who provides and cares more.

You need to balance both sides of the circle. I have met seasoned business owners clinging to a model where their clients no longer want what they offer. The market is in decline but they hold on to an outdated model hoping something will change. I have also met businesses where they only focus on making money and apply no love or skill. As the world becomes increasingly transparent with social media and review sites, poor products and services have no place to hide.

> *Being selective is paramount. Staying focused is crucial.*
> *The Intersect = Your Niche*

Ultimately, your only viable strategy is to exist in the overlap between the two circles. This defines your niche, the market where you are positioned to serve your customers better than anybody else. Here you have a real chance of achieving competitive advantage. Having found your niche, you also need to make sure that you stand out from anybody else in the marketplace, and organise yourself to best exploit your point of difference.

Summarised from Chapter 7:

- *USP* – a unique selling point, you highlight your unique offer
- *Differentiation* – you offer something better and different
- *Competitive advantage* – the way you differentiate yourself is:
    - valued by your customers
    - hard for others to copy to ensure your difference is lasting
- *Core Competence* – how you are organised around your essential difference

Taglines: expressing your competitive advantage to your customers

It is essential to have competitive advantage, but you also need this to translate into sales. For this your customers need to understand the value it delivers to them. This is where a well written tagline comes in. A great tagline should quickly and simply convey why you are different and better than your competition. Your tagline should capture this expression in a simple sentence. There should be no doubt about what you do. Some of these examples may have evolved since they were written, but they still capture the essence of the company's core:

- BMW – The ultimate driving machine
- IKEA – Stylish furniture at low prices for young families
- Volvo – Safe, durable cars

If you truly have competitive advantage and your competitors steal it, they should fail to deliver on your claim. At the time IKEA arrived on the market, how many companies could truly deliver the same promise of stylish furniture at low prices for young families?

Of course, you also need to deliver on your promises. A famous company had the tagline *The world's favourite airline* during a period when it was beset by strikes, delays and arguably outdated customer service. The mismatch between the promise and reality may have done more harm than good.

Scanning and SWOT analysis

In 1941, the Japanese naval fleet decimated the US Navy at Pearl Harbour in a surprise air attack. Some experts believe that preceding the attack there was ample information regarding Japanese activity. However, the significance of that information was ignored, resulting in the US Navy remaining unprepared. Scanning for intelligence is just as relevant for businesses as it is for the military. You need to identify upcoming issues, and decide if they might cause you harm or provide a brilliant opportunity.

In business, you need to accurately interpret the significance of the changes around you. Having established your competitive advantage, you need to look beyond yourself and your customers and anticipate changes in your wider environment. Scanning should be done at least annually, and the resulting considerations built into your business plan.

The aims of the scanning process are:

1 To understand your world and to create an appropriate strategy to compete in it

2 To create appropriate goals so you feel motivated to win

3 To monitor changes in your world, so you can adapt as necessary

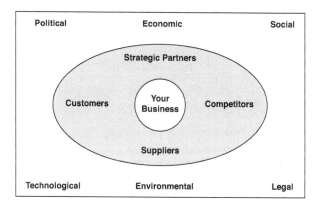

The PESTEL model

There are numerous models for scanning the business environment. This model is comprehensive but easy to remember. It shows:

- Your organisation
- Your inner marketing environment:
  - Customers
  - Competitors
  - Suppliers
  - Strategic partners
- Your outer marketing environment:
  - Political
  - Economic
  - Social
  - Technological
  - Environmental
  - Legal

More complex models include other parties in the inner marketing environment such as investors, stakeholders, trade bodies, unions, press, PR and special interest groups.

SWOT analysis

To apply this to your own business and consider how you will fare in the world at large, you might apply a process called SWOT analysis.

Internal factors – inside your business:

Strengths – what you do well

Weaknesses – what you do badly

External factors – everything else that might affect you:

Opportunities – where you might prosper

Threats – where you may be at risk

You need to apply SWOT to each area of the PESTEL model, as in the example below, asking:

Where are we strong? What do we do well?

Where are we weak? What do we do badly?

What are the opportunities? Where might we prosper?

What are the threats? Where might we be at risk?

Note: In this example, only key issues have been highlighted for clarity.

	Strengths	Weaknesses
Your Business	*New product development*	*High staff turnover*
Inner Environment	**Opportunities**	**Threats**
Customers	*Launch new product Apr XX*	
Competitors	*Emphasise: our brand is market leader*	*3 new competitors in marketplace this year*
Suppliers		
Strategic Partners		
Outer Environment	**Opportunities**	**Threats**
Political		
Economical		
Social		*Existing customers getting married = reduced spend*
Technological	*Battery life increasing*	
Environmental	*New product is green!*	
Legal		*Competition working around our patent*

Planning your future
The long-term plan – circa 10 years

As a business owner, you need a sense of where your business is going. This allows short term decisions and plans to be made. A long-term perspective means that options which may look attractive can be ruled in or out if they serve or distract from your long-term objectives.

You need to decide:

- What are the long-term goals for you and your business?
- What kind of business are you in and where do you want it to go?
- Are you in it:
  - For fame and/or fortune?
  - To pursue your passion?
  - Because you do not enjoy working for others and want to work for yourself?
  - To provide jobs and security for friends and family?
  - To make a difference to your community or society?
  - Or any combination of the above?

Which type of business are you running?

- Self employed, giving you independence and adequate earnings
- Lifestyle business, offering you, and your staff, a better quality of life and income
- Passion based business, earning an income doing what you truly love
- Entrepreneurial business, highly driven to achieve acclaim and/or financial success
- Scalable growth business, intending to grow to a considerable size
- Investor business, developing and selling for significant profit

Where do you want the business to go?

- Sold for a profit
- Passed on to family
- Taken over by existing staff/management
- Closing on the retirement of key managers

This does not have to be an exact plan but, a little like retirement planning, the better your sense of your end goal, the more likely you are to achieve it.

The medium-term plan – circa three to five years

With the long-term goal in mind, what is the nearest mid-term stage that you can clarify? You do not need this to be fleshed out in full detail. It may evolve and change with time, but the greater your clarity for the medium term, the clearer you will be with your immediate plans to get you there.

The short-term plan – circa one to two years

With your longer term aims understood, you need to think through your priorities for the year ahead, aligned with these goals. This is where you get into your short-term plan, normally based on one or two years, and comprising diagnosis of your Business Jet Engine® and a simple business plan.

How much detail?

You need to find a balance between the time spent planning, and putting those plans into action. You need to keep your efforts proportional. You have to balance planning your route and actually flying your route. In addition, the world is constantly changing. Any plan runs the risk of becoming outdated the moment it is written. This risk is especially true for small businesses, where owners are often heavily embroiled in the business itself.

Your plan is a work in progress. It should focus the actions of you and your team. Write the least you can to create clarity so everyone knows what needs to be done. If you are raising finance, you may need a more comprehensive business plan to show investors, but that is not the intention of this book. A plan for investors is not your working document. Keep your plan simple, clear and concise. Focus on key facts. Lay out information so it is quick to read and refer to; especially targets, goals, and project deadlines. And consider how performance and progress will be measured.

This leads on to our next subject of KPIs and measuring and monitoring progress.

Business Planning Diagnostic Questions

Vision/mission & company values

How well:

Have you agreed and articulated your vision and mission statement?

Does your team understand these?

Do they create focus, motivation and passion?

Do your company values and behaviour align with them?

Do your vision, mission & values permeate everything you do?

Customer values and competitive advantage

How well do you:

Clearly identify your ideal and most profitable client base?

Truly understand your customers' values, needs, wants, desires?

Ensure you are uniquely skilled to meet their needs and wants?

Have a plan to attract and retain them?

Identify your niche, where you are strongly positioned?

Clearly differentiate yourself from your competition?

Offer something that your clients can't get elsewhere?

Ensure your competitive advantage is rare or hard to copy?

Ensure your competitive advantage truly adds value to your customer?

Ensure your core competences strengthen your competitive advantage?

Express your difference so it is easily understood by clients and staff?

SWOT analysis (Strengths, Weaknesses, Opportunities, Threats)

How well do you know:

What is happening in the market place?

What other major forces are at play?

Where you are headed and where you want to be?

What might put you out of business in one, three or ten years' time?

What might strengthen your position in one, three or ten years' time?

How well have you identified:

Your own strengths and weaknesses?

Your main competitors strengths and weaknesses?

The opportunities and threats:

Within your inner market environment?

Within your wider market environment (PESTEL)?

Planning/business overview objectives

How well have you established your:

Long-term goals (ten year plan)?

Medium-term goals (three to five year plan)?

Short-term goals (one to two year plan)?

How well have you:

Summarised these in a one to two page document?

Created departmental plans?

Identified the people required to deliver these?

Identified your top strategic priorities using
   The Business Jet Engine®?

Identified the obstacles which are or will prevent
   you achieving them?

Identified the resources which may be required for
   achieving your goals?

Translated these into written SMART goals or projects?

Identified timeframes, costs, obstacles and risks etc?

Translated these into quarterly goals?

Translated these into your first monthly tasks?

KPIs and Measuring and Monitoring Progress

Imagine flying overnight from London to New York in your jet airline. You have completed careful planning for the trip. You have booked-in all your passengers, worked out your flight plan, loaded fuel and supplies needed for the duration, checked the weather, and all staff and passengers are on board. You start your engines and wait for runway clearance. Once given, you roar down the runway, take off, and bear towards the North Atlantic and the night sky.

The hard work done, you can at last sit back, relax, and let the plane do the work. All you need to do now is trust the crew to do their job looking after passengers, and fly in roughly the right direction and all will be well . . .

And that, of course, would be a total fantasy! Even with auto-pilot, and a flight plan loaded into a navigation computer, a pilot will be given many route and altitude changes with more direct routings, earlier climbs and speed increases. At cruising altitude pilots will still be given further route, altitude and radio frequency changes. In addition, the pilot will be monitoring navigation and position, aircraft systems, en route weather and suitable airports for any unexpected landings.

In other words, during flight, there is constant activity measuring and monitoring progress. Critical onboard systems and the outer environment are frequently checked for important changes that may affect the flight. Yet so many businesses fly blind on their own journeys with inadequate planning, and a scarce or total lack of measuring and monitoring progress.

With most business owners working long and stressful hours, literally giving their life-energy to their businesses, it seems crazy to give so much unless it leads to success. The answer, of course, is to have carefully considered key performance indicators that show exactly where you are.

Which KPIs, or what to measure and monitor?

In an ideal world, you would have KPIs to measure and monitor every part of your Business Jet Engine®. However, for most SME businesses, this is unrealistic due to a lack of resource. Instead, you need to apply the 80/20 rule, covered in Chapter 6, and ask yourself what are the smallest elements of your business you can measure to provide the most useful information.

The idea is to identify what you can measure least frequently, with the least effort, and is simplest to analyse whilst providing the best insight into the health of your business. If you have few existing measures the danger is to go overboard and introduce too many measurements at once. What then happens is they take too much time to implement. Recording information becomes a burden, inputting data becomes erratic. Nobody has time to stop and analyse results. Without an obvious and reliable benefit to the process, motivation decreases, until all recording stops.

If you are a larger business with dedicated staff running each department, then it is easier to establish more KPIs. Decide on a realistic number of KPIs for each department, maybe three to five that they work with on a regular basis. Only the critical KPIs are then reported back to you.

Choosing your KPIs depends on your business, and what drives it.

It also depends on the areas in which you are most vulnerable or weak, or where you are focusing for growth. Use your Business Jet Engine® to help you establish this. It may be that the three areas you have chosen to fix or improve for the year ahead are also the areas where KPIs will prove most useful.

Although many businesses are working with inadequate financial KPIs, and this would often be an obvious place to start, there can be exceptions. For example, I work with businesses where cashflow is exceptionally healthy, but growth is proving a challenge. In this case, although I would normally recommend accurate cash flow forecasts as a priority (running out of cash being the number one business killer), they decided to focus on establishing marketing and sales targets.

Example KPI shortlist

There is no definitive list of KPIs to build from, but for most SMEs, this is a good place to start:

Customers
Customer satisfaction
Repeat business
Referrals

People
Staff grading/performance
Staff satisfaction

Finance
Cashflow forecast
Profit and loss
Balance sheet
Budget/Projected sales and expenses

Marketing
List sign-up and unsubscribe rates
ROI (return on investment) on sign-ups

Sales

Sales targets

Sales conversions

Average order value

Customer lifetime value

Quality

Returns, rejects or re-work

Planning

Annual SWOT analysis

Choose your top three KPIs to trial, which may correlate to your three Business Jet Engine® improvement areas. Implement these and use on a regular basis, for example, over six months. Then build your list of KPIs to five, then eight in total. Once these eight are proving their value and are being used consistently, build on your next areas for growth, or where you feel you are also vulnerable.

Additional KPIs may include:

Operations

Inventory turnover

Project performance against quotes

Capacity utilisation

Order fulfilment

Sales & Marketing

Revenue breakdown by customer

Revenue breakdown by service/product type

Revenue sources – lead generation information

Client and referral channels – social media, website, forums etc.

New business *vs* repeat *vs* referral ratios

Number of referrals by source

Funnel drop-off rate

Market share

Financial Indicators

Profitability/gross profit margin as a percentage of sales

Revenue growth rate

Solvency – current ratio

Gearing – debt to equity ratio

Work-in progress – WIP turnover

Debtor days

Fixed costs – fixed cost ratio

Variable costs – gross margin

Performance against budget and cost – variance reviews

Costs as a % of revenue – payroll, advertising & marketing etc.

Costs per employee – rent, stationery, travel, phone etc.

Accounts payable turnover

Staff

A-player hiring success rate

A-player retention rate

ROI (return on investment) on training

Profit per employee

Sales per employee (annual sales/number of full-time equivalent staff)

Absenteeism

Business Performance Indicators

Performance against service level agreements

Quality of product or service

Response rates, enquiries to customer resolution

ROI (return on investment) ie capital equipment, new staff, marketing

Accuracy of estimates/reporting – corporation tax, VAT, payroll, etc

Number of compliance breeches

Capacity *vs* actual production

Ideal timeframes for measuring and monitoring KPIs

The principles to apply are covered more fully in Chapter 13; The Importance of Timely Reviews. In brief, to establish the appropriate timeframe for both taking and reviewing measurements, the key factor is the rate of change of that area. How quickly is your business and environment changing? The more rapidly change is occurring, the more frequently you should take measurements and review.

Ask yourself:

- What is the time frame within which too little will have changed?
- What is the time frame after which too much will have changed?

Your ideal interval is probably somewhere in the middle. Test it, trial it and assess if you have sufficient time to adjust to critical changes. See if you can measure and review less frequently, or whether more frequent intervals are required to stay in control of developments.

Having proved the value of any KPI, automate the process wherever possible. This will minimise the resources you commit to the benefits of essential information.

KPIs Diagnostic Questions

Measuring & monitoring progress

How well have you established the measurable targets/KPIs for each department for:

Customers?

Products?

Customer service?

Operations?

Marketing?

Finance?

People?

Overall business progress?

How well:

Do you record, monitor and evaluate them?

Do relevant staff understand these targets for their
  departments?

Are relevant staff motivated by these targets for
  their departments?

Do relevant staff take responsibility for achieving their targets?

Do you take action to remedy issues and keep on track?

Section Summary

What you have learned

- Some of the more expert concepts for each part of The Business Jet Engine®
- Where you are weak or strong against those concepts
- What you may need to learn or improve next

Tips

- Match your use of this section to your requirements:
  - Quick insight
  - To be more thorough
  - If you are unsure how to improve a weak area

Required actions from this section

- Read the relevant chapters or sub-headings
- Score yourself using the advanced diagnostic questions
- Decide what you need to develop and how you will do it

In the next chapter

- Learn the mindset of winners

Section 4

Flying High
and keeping it all going

This section is about taking your knowledge and experience beyond the aims of this book and giving you shortcuts to some of the great information available to speed your learning and development.

In this section you will learn:

- The importance of a winning mindset
- Key principles of leadership
- The importance of timely reviews

Find guidance on further useful information such as:

- The Business Jet Engine® online resources
- Recommended reading

CHAPTER TWELVE

The Mindset of Winners

The aim of this chapter is to explain

- The importance of mindset
- How your thoughts influence your actions
- The value of aiming for your ideal

Tips

For each concept, ask yourself:
- How well do I apply this in my own business and life?
- How could I do this better?
- How well do my team apply this in my business?
- How could I help them do this better?

Actions

- Think how each concept applies to you and your team
- Consider how to apply each concept more fully

Have you ever noticed that it is not always the most talented person who becomes most successful? Have you ever mastered an activity such as golf, art or a musical instrument which you struggled with at the start while others found it easy? As the years went on your peers gave up where you continued. The more time passed, the better you became, and those who decided to quit got left behind. Or were you ever the talented one that gave up and watched your peers keep going to success?

Many top achievers report this. At the start of their careers they were not the most talented, but they focused on their goals, they continued while more talented competition became disheartened or distracted and finally stopped. Those that continued, improved, step-by-step, until they reached their goal.

What separates those that continue from those that give up is mindset. Below I cover the key concepts that can make the greatest difference.

Clarity of Outcome

Have you ever been driving your car, when you notice a large pot-hole you would like to avoid? You keep staring at it, determined to miss it. The next thing you know, THUMP! You have driven over it. If so, there is a key principle at play.

You get what you focus on!

Many of you will be familiar with this idea, but if you are not, I suggest you start to give it attention. The more you play with the idea, the more you will find it to be true – for both good and bad outcomes – in business and in life.

Just like you focused on the object on the road, and found you had steered into it, the same is true of both your conscious and unconscious goals. It works a bit like a heat seeking missile, or a plane on a flight path. Whether you intend to or not, you tend to work towards whatever most occupies your mind. Sooner or later you find you have created what you focused on.

'Why don't all my dreams come true?' you may ask. 'I'm always thinking about money/what I need/success etc. Why don't I have more of it?'

This is because, along with your goals, you also have powerful un-conscious aims and objectives. These may be directed toward the opposite of what you want, like your lack of money/needs fulfilled or success. If they are more powerful than a weak wish, you tend to achieve those instead. For example you may have the wish to get fit but equally you have a much greater desire to eat and watch television. The greater desire will be the goal that wins.

You may have a goal to be financially successful, which may require new actions and risks. But you may have an unconscious goal to stay in your comfort zone. Again, the more powerful goal will win. To raise your chance of success, your goals need to be clear, powerful and compelling; more so than those that could pull you the opposite way.

Positive Outlook

Just as you tend to get what you focus on, the same is true of your attitude. If this is a negative attitude, you tend to create negative results. If you have a positive attitude, you more often create positive results. Psychological studies have proved this, but your own observations should show that positive people more frequently get what they want.

If you tend toward negativity, try and give more energy and attention to the positive outcomes you achieve. Remember the 80/20 rule. Even if little seems to work for you, just keep building on the small part that does. Great things will come from it if you persist . . .

Persistence

At the start of this chapter, we discussed how it is not always the most initially talented person who becomes the most successful. Many top athletes report that in the early stages of their careers they were not the best in their field. There were others who could naturally out-perform them. The big difference was that some people gave up, whilst our champion stuck with their discipline until they reached the top. Like walking up a mountain, most of us can reach the top if we pace ourselves for the distance, rest or reduce our stride if we need to when the going gets tough, but stay focused and keep going towards our end goal.

What can make persistence hard is when you fear a goal will remain out of reach. This is when you must accurately assess whether a goal is beyond your current skill set, and what that goal really means to you. Is it worth investing in raising your game to that higher level? There is ample evidence of what humans can achieve when they set their minds to it, even against incredible odds. The question is, how much do your dreams really matter, and are they right for you?

Flexibility

Just as you need to have the courage to persist and stay focused on your goals, you also need to know when to stop, reassess your position and be flexible in your approach. Sometimes all you need is a break and to come back to the situation refreshed, when your way forward will become clear.

At other times, what you really need to do is consider a new goal, or attempt a fresh angle. How could you get the same result in a completely different way?

Life is full of paradoxes, and this is certainly one of them. Knowing whether you need to persist, or try something different, can be one of the hardest decisions. Often your only solution is to try both and see which allows you the greatest progress.

Having Faith in the Design Approach

One of the most important concepts I learnt in my first career as a product designer is what I now call the *design approach*. When someone needs a solution, what they often do is explore the solutions that currently exist. Then choose one of them. You could call this going for *known* or *convenient solutions*.

By contrast, designers think of their ideal solution, how they would like it to look, to feel, to work. They may not know how to achieve this end, but they are clear what perfection looks like and they persist towards it. They have faith and trust that if they stay true to their design and the design process, they will come across the right technology, people and know-how. They may not achieve their 100% ideal, but they will get 80–90% of the way towards it, which is far closer than simply going for a known or convenient solution.

This concept is similar to when you have chosen a destination for a holiday, but know little about that place. From making the decision to go, you come across all sorts of useful information that inspires you; through articles online, in magazines, programmes on television and people who have been there. All of these shape your knowledge and ideas for when you get there.

This design approach can be applied to your priorities and goals, in both business and life. This requires having faith in your ideals – and remaining alert to the solutions that appear along the way.

What you have learned

- Mindset plays a large part in success
- Have clear goals
- Stay positive, focused and determined
- Be flexible when your approach is not working
- Have faith in your ideal. You will get at least 80% towards it!

Tips

For each concept, ask yourself:
- How well do I apply this in my own business and life?
- How could I do this better?
- How well do my team apply this in my business?
- How could I help them do this better?

Required actions from this chapter

- Think how each concept applies to you and your team
- Consider how to apply each concept more fully

In the next chapter

- Learn key principles of leadership to execute your plans

CHAPTER THIRTEEN

Leadership Principles

The aim of this chapter is to explain

- Key concepts of leadership to help you:
  - Follow clear steps to deliver your plans
  - Align around more meaningful goals
  - Create time to take action
  - Keep others accountable for success
  - Use the power of repeatable systems

Tips

- Ask yourself for each concept:
  - How well do I apply this in my business?
  - How could I do this better?
  - How well do my team apply this?
  - How could I help them do this better?

Actions

- Think how each concept applies to you and your team
- Consider how to apply each concept more fully

If you have worked through the suggested actions in each chapter of this book you will now have plans for your business. The next challenge is to turn those plans into actions and results, and this comes down to your ability in leadership. In this chapter, you will be introduced to the Seven Essential Tasks of Leadership without which, any project or act of leadership will be less than its best. In addition, you will also cover several salient concepts which come out of the seven tasks; tips for goal setting, prioritisation, managing your time and holding others to account.

The Seven Essential Tasks of Leadership

This section gives you a brief introduction to the seven tasks that need to be present in any act of leadership:

Task 1: Goals and plans, including prioritisation and time management

The first task of leadership is to create your goal and a plan; an intention of where to get to and a sense of how to get there. If this is unclear, then it is your job as leader to ensure this gets clarified, even if you facilitate this through others.

In addition, you need to set priorities to help yourself and others better manage time.

Task 2: Working the plan, habits and streamlining culture

Having established the goal and plan, your next task is to work the plan. For most goals this involves taking action on a consistent basis, doing the same or similar tasks daily, weekly or monthly. If you want to get fit, you may form a pattern of going to the gym three times a week with particular exercises on set days: in business similar tasks get repeated over time to achieve a goal.

What you do consistently becomes your culture.

As you work your plan, your job as leader is to streamline your repetitive actions, to streamline your culture, to most expediently reach your goal.

Task 3: Scanning for meaningful change

Having made your plan, you work your plan – to guaranteed success! Sadly, life rarely works that way, and neither does business. The third leadership task is to have targets, measurements and controls. You need to measure the gap between the target and your current position. You are most likely to be a little bit above or below your target. If you find there is too big a gap then you need to take action to resolve this. This leads us on to the next task.

Task 4: Problem solving

If from your scanning you find you have too big a gap, then you may have a problem. This leads to the leadership task of problem solving. Ironically, we are basically paid to solve problems in life, but few of us are properly taught this. It is too easy to rush to fix the immediate issue without proper consideration, often making things worse in the process. Good problem solvers ensure they fully understand the issue at hand, consider multiple options, then carefully decide on their most promising solution.

Task 5: Implementing – testing, refining, making a part of culture

Having chosen your most likely solution, the next task is to implement that solution. Rather than rush in and apply a hopeful solution right across your business, good problem solvers figure out how to test, prototype and trial a proposed solution to ensure that it works. This gives you the opportunity to refine, adapt and develop it until it works as intended. Only then should you apply it more widely, ensuring consistency, so it becomes part of your culture, part of what you do.

Task 6: Relationships

Throughout the whole process, you need to involve people, from tasks one to five. This starts with identifying the relationships that are required to help you achieve your goal. You then need to nurture, improve or develop those relationships for maximum effect. You also need to identify the relationships that may distract or prevent you from achieving your goal, the relationships you need to diminish or curtail.

Task 7: Influence

Having identified the contacts that will most help you, you need to influence those relationships appropriately and effectively.

Nobody likes to be treated inappropriately. We all have a built-in understanding of how we would like to be approached in any context, a way that we think is either right or wrong. If we are treated inappropriately, we tend to feel angry, resentful, and even consider revenge. When we are treated appropriately we tend to feel benevolent towards that person and more willing to help them towards their goals.

Influencing effectively means that we have clear communication and agreements. It is so much easier to perform well when everyone knows exactly what is expected.

Good leadership

Good leadership requires all seven tasks to take place on a continuous basis. Those who lead well tend to be competent in all seven areas. Poor leaders may be weak in one or two areas, or neglect whole areas all together.

To improve your own leadership, consider the Seven Tasks and ask yourself how well you perform in each area.

- Which tasks do you do well?
- Which tasks could you do better?
- What would change if you improved in each area, especially your weakest?
- What might help you do that?

Make a commitment to being a better leader. However good your plans, it is your leadership ability that will determine whether or not you achieve them!

Having explored the Seven Tasks, further concepts that will support you are:

- Goal-setting, prioritisation and time management
- Getting the best from others by holding them to account
- The importance of timely reviews

We will start with the first, goal-setting, prioritisation and time management.

Goal Setting

Goal setting is part of the first leadership task and central to all achievement. Alongside applying The Business Jet Engine® model, these tips will help you with goal setting in general.

Goal setting top tips

See the bigger picture

Any goal worth setting needs to be part of a bigger plan. How does it serve your one, three and ten year plans and improve your situation?

Make it exciting. Make it matter

People tend to take the greatest action towards goals with the biggest rewards, and avoid those that present the greatest threats. Tune in to your fears to be aware of what causes you to procrastinate. Tap in to your desires to create motivation and momentum.

Make it measurable

You need to know what success looks like so you can recognise it when you achieve it. Make it measurable and measure progress towards it.

Think through the steps

Think of the end result and work backwards. What actions do you need to take to reach your goal? Think through the what, why, how, who, where, when, how much, at what cost in time, money *and* energy, and at what risk.

Celebrate success along the way

It is easy to think that the only time to celebrate is when the main goal is achieved. In the meantime, you and your team can lose drive and focus. Celebrating smaller gains, even in a small way, can reinvigorate you and remind you what you are doing and why. Winning feels good. When you win, you want to do it again, so catch yourself winning.

Make a schedule

Time in the diary is worth more than *'someday'* in the mind. Schedule time to do the tasks to reach your goals.

Prioritise

We all have too much to do. Not all of it is worthwhile. Know what really makes the difference and what does not. Learn the 80/20 rule and live by it.

– Identify what you give time to that does not reward you anymore and cut it out.
– Identify what gives you the greatest reward, prioritise it and do it more.

Avoid distractions

Write down your ten big distractions. Feel good when you say no to them.

Know yourself

Pay attention to what helps you work well and build your prime work-time around it.

Remember SMART goals . . .

They need to be:

Specific

Measurable

Assignable

Realistic

Time-related

Prioritisation, Time Management and Putting Time Aside

The biggest challenge with strategic goals is that they require effort in addition to your day-to-day tasks. They require time that can be hard to find; time carved out on top of your normal activities. Finding this time only happens when you recognises the importance of your strategic goals in relation to your long-term success. At that point, you see them as of equal or greater priority than your everyday tasks.

Parkinson's law is the adage that:

'Work expands to fill the time available for its completion.'

This can be especially true of everyday tasks. The risk is that they may be completed to a higher standard than required, done at a more leisurely pace, or are simply allowed to take up more time than they truly deserve.

To aid with appropriate prioritisation, Stephen Covey's quadrants, summarised below, are extremely useful, followed by some general time-management top tips.

Time management – Stephen Covey's quadrants

Written in 1989, Stephen Covey's book The Seven Habits of Highly Effective People describes four quadrants which have become widely respected as a task prioritisation tool. The idea is that tasks follow two dimensions of urgency and importance.

These dimensions can be used to form a matrix:

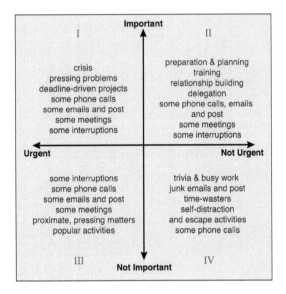

Over focus in one quadrant may result in:

Quadrant I: Stress, burnout, crisis management, always putting out fires

Quadrant 2: Vision, perspective, balance, discipline, control, few crises

Quadrant 3: Short-term focus, continual crisis management, feeling victimised or out-of-control

Quadrant 4: Ineffectiveness, irresponsibility, achieving nothing of value

The objective of the quadrants is to raise awareness of what tasks are most important to the long-term future of the company and to plan time and tasks accordingly:

Quadrants 1 & 2:

– Be efficient in quadrant 1 tasks and return to quadrant 2 as soon as possible

– Focus on quadrant 2 tasks – achieve them before they become quadrant 1

Quadrants 3 & 4:
- Delegate or minimise quadrant 3 tasks
- Delete or remove quadrant 4 tasks wherever possible

Time management top tips

Do not be driven by your email inbox!
> Check at intervals only.

Ask yourself better questions
> What is the most important thing to achieve this year, month, day, hour, minute?
>
> What am I doing now?
>
> What problem am I really trying to solve?
>
> Is this the best way of doing it?
>
> Who could help?
>
> Is this the best use of my time?
>
> What is really most important to me in my work and life?

Put your top three goals on a sticky note each day
> Write it out the night before, plus three key 'nice to have' minor goals.

Think through your system. Make it right for you and keep it simple
> Use lists, calendars, planners and alarms that fit the flow of your work.
>
> Use reminders.
> - Place them in a location that will remind you at the right time.
>   - Sticky note by car keys of task to perform when leaving work.
> - Use alarms, notes, actual items.
>
> Use checklists.
> - Especially recurring tasks, e.g. travel, exhibitions, presentations etc.
>
> Use technology only when it helps.
> - Are you 'fiddling' with IT or achieving the work?

Know Yourself. What suits your nature and your work?

    Are you rational, visual, physical, emotional or digital?

    Know what causes you to procrastinate.

      – It is nearly always fear.

    Know what you use to distract yourself.

      – It is nearly always something you want/prefer.

Leave space in your diary

    There will always be unexpected items that crop up.

Know when to say 'No'

    Will saying 'yes' and failing cause more harm than good?

Know when to delegate

    Who is the expert?

    Who is most appropriate to solve this?

    Know when it is someone else's problem and should stay that way.

    Train your support.

    Take the time to develop expertise around you. It pays long-term.

Start big tasks in plenty of time and pace yourself for the long haul

    Work in stages. Allow your unconscious to do the work.

    Know what work you will do best and when.

    Manage your energy and stay healthy.

      – Take breaks, especially lunch.

      – Get exercise and rest.

      – Watch what you eat.

      – Moderate your consumption of caffeine and alcohol.

    Keep it in perspective.

    How good does this have to be?

    What is appropriate?

    What will happen if you do not do it?

Breathe

> Our work is generally better when we have a calm, clear head. Slow, relaxed, deep breathing calms our whole nervous system, telling it that any moment of stress has passed.
>
> Our body and mind relaxes, allowing a better long-term performance.

How to Hold Your Team Members to Account

Alongside managing yourself and your time, one of the greatest challenges is managing others. There are many principles which apply to doing this well:

- Delegation
- Communication
- Motivation
- Teamwork
- Training & development
- Reviews & appraisals

For the purposes of this book, I want to focus on just one concept that may prove of greatest value: the art of holding your team members to account.

The myth of the Lone Hero

Very few leaders achieve success on their own. However, most of us have grown up with the *myth of the lone hero*, James Bond, Dirty Harry, Rambo or Wolverine. Heroes that make their own rules and defy the odds. They beat the bad-guy, save the world, and win the girl. Most of all, they work alone.

Despite the myth, the hero's approach rarely works for mere mortals. Most truly successful people use the power of teams. They engage the hearts and minds of others to help them realise their dreams and they use experts as much as they can. They are focused on achievement by the fastest route, which means they don't do it all themselves. Yet because of the myth, too many leaders have grown up with the belief they need to do it all. No-one else can be trusted.

They either fail to delegate or delegate badly, by micro-managing or only checking progress at the last moment. Neither scenario produces a good result. The first approach results in the leader being drained and pre-occupied and team members feeling constrained. The second results in deadlines being missed, especially if the team is inexperienced.

A better approach requires thoughtful but timely contact, allowing the leader to check-in at appropriate intervals, and means team members own tasks and have to think for themselves.

> *If you are unable to delegate a task*
> *it is a clue that your team requires more training.*

Here are some tips to help you hold your team members to account.

Making team members accountable top tips

First ensure that your team members fully understand the required goal or task. Use the planning questions to help you with this:

- **What:** The central idea, the task, the objective.
- **Why:** Why this is important.
- **How:** The way you hope it might be done.
- **Who:** Who you expect to be involved.
- **Where:** The location of key events.
- **When:** The critical points in time when you expect key stages to be complete.
- **How Much:** The degree to which it is done, hours spent, quantities required, etc.
- **At What Cost:** The resource to be gained or used up: often money, but it could be time, energy, emotions, relationships.
- **At What risk:** What could jeopardise success? Is there anything mission-critical they should know?

You need to agree with your team what success looks like, and any sub-goals and milestones. What do they need to achieve and by when? When will you review progress to maintain a healthy rhythm? A common reason that teams do not achieve their goals is that targets are not set or progress reviewed. Remember the phrase: what gets measured gets done.

Accountability/coaching questions – the basics

By helping others to think through their challenges, find their own solutions and decide their next steps, you are coaching them to take ownership of their tasks, rather than leaving it all to you. Not only that, but by moving in that direction, you encourage them to start acting like a leader by taking responsibility and thinking for themselves. At this point, the following Chinese Proverb seems appropriate:

> *'Tell me and I will forget,*
> *show me and I may remember,*
> *involve me and I will understand.'*

The following sequence of questions is a simple yet powerful way to coach your team and hold them to account for their tasks. Use the optional questions should the validity of the goal or project need to be re-evaluated.

Questions in bold hold the highest value:

1. **What is the task/project?**
   a   What shall we call it?
2. **Where are you at, out of 10?**
   a   **What is the missing 'X'?** E.g. If the first answer is 7/10, the missing 'X' is 3/10.
   b   What would make it a 10?
3. **What is your biggest obstacle?**
   a   How do you propose overcoming it?
   b   What other options do you have?
   c   Who could you ask/could help, who has solved this before or is an expert?

Optional Questions

4 What is the problem you are *really* trying to solve?

    a What does success look like?

    b What will that give you?

    c What is the benefit?

Optional Questions

5 Why is this really worth solving?

    a What will that be worth in time, money and energy?

    b Especially, what is this worth financially?

6 What is your specific next step?

    a **What will that get you to out of 10?**

    b How will we measure it?

    c **When will you get there?**

7 When shall we meet again to review this?

The Importance of Timely Reviews

We have looked at the importance of creating plans, engaging people through leadership to deliver those plans and good systems and processes to ensure repeat activities are effective. All of this activity can be fruitless if you do not stop to check that it is taking you where you want to go.

Imagine you take-off in your plane, lift smoothly into the air, reach cruising altitude, put the plane on auto-pilot, recline your seat and relax, knowing in eight hours you'll be in New York. Eight hours later, you look out of the window. All you can see is ice, stretching to the horizon. You check your navigation systems, but nothing is working. The screen has gone blank. Slowly you realise, you are lost, low on fuel, and supplies are running low . . .

Pressing on without checking

Clearly, you would not want to be in that situation. Yet so many businesses press on regardless. A major obstacle is the feeling that time spent measuring progress, creating reports and attending reviews could be time spent producing work. It takes you away from the core activity that earns you money. In addition, organisations plagued by reports are notorious for passing paper, person-to-person, and achieving little.

A balance needs to be struck between pressing-on with necessary work, and making sure that:

* Your activities are taking you in the direction you want to go
* You are making the progress required to reach your target in time

Great progress, wrong direction

As with our aircraft example, there is no point making great progress in the wrong direction. You need to know where you are headed and that your activities point you in the right direction.

Perfect Windows Ltd – Example 1

A firm works overtime to get a replacement window project complete. They deliver on time, but with no established quality controls; the original specification is only checked when the windows arrive on site. At this point the team realise the glass should be tinted. The whole project has to be returned to their workshop, glass re-ordered, windows stripped down, new glass re-assembled and brought back to the client site. The ensuing re-work, damage to their reputation and extended project time cost the business far more than the original project was worth. If it had established quality procedures to check the project against the original brief, the error could have been picked up before the project went off-course.

Focus Associates – Example 2

A consultancy wants to increase revenue to £1M per annum within five years. It drives hard to acquire new clients. The focus is on getting clients, as many as possible, as fast as possible. They invest heavily in their sales and marketing process to achieve this and manage this well. It is only at the end of year one that anyone stops, analyses and reviews progress. Everyone is delighted to have gained 50 clients and an increased turnover of £125k, but each client is only worth about £2.5k in projects per year. That means the business has to gain, service, and maintain 400 clients a year to attain £1M in revenue, a near impossible task even with more staff. This would be a high volume, low value model which the business is not set up to operate.

If the team had focused on winning £20k clients, which they have competitive advantage in servicing, they would only need about 50 clients per year. This is a higher value, lower volume market, which they could realistically cater for, but requiring a different sales and marketing approach. Instead, they have built a sales machine which cannot attract the desired client base.

Right direction, progress unknown

You may be confident that you are headed in the right direction. But you also need to check your rate of progress. Will you get there in an appropriate timeframe?

GamingSoft – Example 1

A company that provides outsourced gaming software has a revenue target of £500k. It has a great market reputation, wins repeat business due to the quality of work, and everyone in the firm is keen that this continues. Due to their pride in their business and the team's great expertise, they ensure that every project is completed to the highest possible standard, often including modifications and requests for extra features from their clients as they progress. However, no-one is recording project time, and additional work is not being properly costed against the job. On a monthly basis, profit and loss is not being measured or analysed. Although at year end they hit their turnover target of £500k, when they produced their management accounts they could see that any profit had been eaten up by the extra project time and the overheads of the business. It also meant they did not have time for their strategic goals as they were always flat-out on projects.

On reflection, the business owners wished that they applied better time-recording, and produced monthly profit and loss reports. Then they would have been focused on the time a project was really taking and been more strict charging clients for additions to the brief. By not properly measuring progress, they had a false sense of security that they were making a profit, when in fact they were falling short.

Bright Spark Ltd – Example 2

An audio-visual contractor has a national presence, with a central HQ and five satellite offices. Each office is run by an office manager with responsibility for the success of their team. In January, office managers identify three strategic areas they would like to improve, so their office performs at its best. They submit this as a plan, with key tasks and timescales, to HQ for approval. Their plan needs to fit within an overall strategy set by HQ, but allows the managers a good degree of autonomy. So far, so good. But once the year is underway, both offices and HQ are busy. No-one at HQ checks progress at the offices or holds the office managers to account. Office managers stay focused on the day-to-day tasks delivering projects to their customers. Unsurprisingly, only a fraction of the strategic tasks get done, with less than 40% complete. This process repeats year-on-year.

This is how many businesses operate. They have good intentions, but without accountability and regular reviews, plans get forgotten and projects remain incomplete. The chance to get on a better footing gets lost. The strategic plan remains a wish, not a plan, and even though there is a sense of heading in the right direction, there is no significant improvement, year after year.

Choosing the right timeframe for reviews

If reviews are important, what is the best timeframe? The key factor here is the rate of change. How quickly is your business moving and how quickly do other factors that may affect you also change? The more rapidly things occur, the more frequently you should measure and review.

Like a car on a motorway, as your speed and rate of change increase you need to check your mirrors more often – and look further ahead.

If you have thousands of sales via the internet in a day, you probably want hourly or daily reporting. If you run two or three predictable projects a year, quarterly reporting may suffice, while project progress may need hourly, daily or weekly reports.

Ask yourself:

- What is the time frame within which too little will have changed?
- What is the time frame after which too much will have changed?

Your interval for reviews is probably somewhere in the middle. Test it, trial it. See if you have enough information, at the right frequency, to adjust to your environment and course-correct in a timely manner.

If you wish to make progress, then it is essential to run timely reviews. Team members need to be held to account, and review dates adhered to. These reviews create the pulse of your engine and the rhythm of your business. When you create better plans, and those plans reach fulfilment, there is no better feeling than flying high!

What you have learned

- There are seven tasks of leadership that work as a cycle
- Clearly defined goals create better team alignment and success
- Strategic goals require time not readily available
- Prioritisation and time management help you make that time
- Big goals need a team
- Teams need accountability and reviews to ensure action
- Coaching helps team members think for themselves
- Timely reviews ensure you reach your goals

Tips

Ask yourself for each concept:

- How well do I apply this in my business?
- How could I do this better?
- How well do my team apply this?
- How could I help them do this better?

Required actions from this chapter

- Think how each concept applies to you and your team
- Consider how to apply each concept more fully

In the next chapter

- Explore how to take things furhter

CHAPTER FOURTEEN

Taking it Further

Having got this far, what next? After investing time to read this book, you may find yourself facing a typical set of conflicting choices. The question is, do any of these scenarios capture where you are and what you are likely to do next?

Four Scenarios

Scenario 1: Forget the book or *return to it repeatedly*

Hopefully, you have learnt a lot from The Business Jet Engine® and you now understand yourself and your business more deeply. But often, having covered a lot of densely packed information, after a few weeks, much of it fades away so you remember only one, two, or three main concepts; the concepts most relevant to your situation. Despite the benefits you have gained, there is a risk that you will put this book on a shelf and forget everything else that is in it, wasting much of the time you have invested.

By contrast, you could choose to re-read this book again at intervals, re-exposing yourself to the material so that the concepts become engrained. The ideas which you first picked up on will become richer as you work with them. And ideas which were less relevant at first, will become more so, as you and your business grow.

Scenario 2: *Change everything at once* or *make planned steady progress*

Feeling motivated by these concepts, you may be inspired with a hundred new projects and want to put them in place immediately. Business owners risk moving from inaction to *all*-action, with too many projects and a work-rate that cannot be sustained.

By contrast, instead of trying to implement all your ideas at once, you could work towards your goals in a planned and sustainable manner with a manageable set of priorities, that generate success, one step at a time.

Scenario 3: *Do everything yourself* or *build a team of support*

You may commit to actioning the many ideas in this book and making sure that your business works at its best, whatever the cost. But if you do, remember the *myth of the lone hero*. In reality, the bigger your business the harder it is to make it alone. You cannot do or know everything. In essence, if you trust no-one to do what you can, this creates a limit to your success.

Instead, share the concepts you have learned. Be like most success-ful people and build a team around you. Find people who will take your problems away and bring them back to you solved, to a standard you no longer have time to achieve personally. Find the best help you can get. Employ people passionate in each field to cover your vital roles. Where necessary, coach, develop and train them to the levels you require. And above all, engage them heart and mind, in the value of sharing the journey and rewards of your end goals.

Scenario 4: *Direct your own learning* or *get professional support*

If you use The Business Jet Engine® as a handbook, it provides many of the tools you need to develop yourself and your plans. Following the process in a structured manner will enable you to make great progress. This will take commitment and dedication to your end goals, but it can be successfully achieved.

Whilst directing your own learning, be sure to research the many sources of information, available in bookstores and online, for each part of The Business Jet Engine®. In addition, at the back of this book, I have made a list of recommended reading material for each area. But remember, different books suit different people, so try and browse or assess the content if you can before buying them, and be sure to find the books that best match your experience and learning style.

Alternatively, you may find it quicker to employ the services of a specialist consultant for the areas in which you most need support. When learning any new skill or subject there is a huge benefit in engaging an expert: not just an expert in that field, but also an expert coach, teacher or mentor. Look for someone who specialises in other people's development and has a structured approach to bring them along that path. There are many excellent coaches and consultants offering their services, so I would suggest that you ask friends or contacts for recommendations with a proven track record. As with any field, the quality and experience of coaches will vary. To ensure you hire the coach who is right for you, try to get a taste of their skills, maybe through a consultation or one-off session. If you can, ideally meet up to three coaches to find the best fit with your personality, expertise, business and budget.

Why try professional business coaching?

A good business coach will help you analyse your business and create a plan to move forward in a focused and structured way. However experienced you are in business, it always helps to have an expert with an outside perspective. When you are in a situation, or too close to a problem, it can be hard to be objective or pick up on certain details. A business coach removes this issue of proximity helping you stand back and look afresh, whilst also bringing their own insight and experience.

To do this, a good coach will listen, observe, question, and challenge; helping you clarify your thinking to form an accurate picture. With this achieved, your coach may introduce examples of best practice for you to consider, or help you explore options to move your situation forward.

Flying High with Martin Riley

There are a number of options if you would like to continue your journey with us . . .

Working with me personally

Having read this book, you may decide that most of all you would like to work with me personally to hone your own Business Jet Engine® to its maximum potential. If this is of interest, you can go to

www.businessjetengine.co.uk

to find out what I offer. Or email us directly to discuss how I can help you to get your business performing at its best:

info@businessjetengine.co.uk.

The Business Jet Engine® website

Whilst personal coaching is the most effective resource for developing bespoke business plans, this may not be a practical solution for your business. The Business Jet Engine® website contains an engaging explanation of the diagnostic model in this book – providing interactive tools, checklists and further questions to aid you in gaining clarity about your current business position. Our simple videos enable you to share key concepts and messages with your leadership team easily and conveniently, ensuring everyone is working towards the same goals.

Online learning is a convenient and diverse method of bringing information to life, especially if you prefer to be shown ideas and talked through the tasks, rather than having to read them. It offers an alternative way of consuming the concepts; combining video, audio, images, text, and digital tools for a multi-faceted approach to working with new information and revisiting best-practice.

Our website offers two high value options:

FREE Bonus Content

Designed to accompany this book, the **FREE Bonus Content** gives a quick overview of The Business Jet Engine®. The animated diagram illustrates each stage of the model in an easy to follow video, while the downloadable diagnostic tools allow you to apply scores directly to your business and quickly see the areas that most need attention.

The Business Jet Engine® Online

In four sections of high quality videos, I explain each step of the diagnostic in a clear conversational manner. The Business Jet Engine® model is built up in stages, whilst simple direction and prompts are provided to help you apply the theory directly to your business. Each section is accompanied by a series of slides and worksheets that can be used to track your progress through the course and record the results seen in your business. Additional interactive tools are offered with this course for a complete business analysis.

The Business Jet Engine® social media

You can find us on a number of social media channels including Twitter, Facebook and Youtube.

We will be sharing stories from business owners like you about how The Business Jet Engine® book and online tools have helped them to grow and achieve their goals. You will also find additional tips and advice for creating simple but effective changes in your business. Additionally, find details of events where we'll be speaking or holding workshops – and keep an eye out for our live events!

We would love to hear your own business success stories – email us at **info@businessjetengine.co.uk**

So please join us and look out for exciting updates in the future . . .

twitter.com/BusJetEng

facebook.com/businessjetengine

youtube.com/businessjetengine

Have a Great Flight . . .

Having travelled with you this far. I would like to thank you for reading this book. It has taken me two years to write, and it has been many, many more years in the making. Both developing the tools and the confidence to bring them to fruition. We are all on a journey, myself included. I set out so long ago on my own hero's adventure in the hope that somehow I could make a difference. From my first career in design, evolving into my career in coaching, I've always wanted to create something that really mattered, that could make life easier and better. A model that has proved itself of great value to my clients will now hopefully be of value to you.

Perhaps you have gained important insights and approaches from this book. For some, I may have saved you from costly mistakes or years of painful learning. For others, I may have sharpened your knowledge in a few key areas and shown you the simplest of ways to plan your route forward. For those already honed by experience, I may have highlighted a few gaps in your knowledge, confirmed how much you already know or that your knowledge exceeds the scope of this book. But even if that is the case, you now have a simple but powerful tool to share your wisdom and work with your team.

Most importantly, I hope I have helped you clarify what you most want to achieve with your business, both emotionally and financially. By understanding yourself and your business more clearly, I hope you will be flying high and speeding across the skies on the way to your dreams!

Wishing you the very best of journeys,

Bibliography – Recommended Reading

Innovation and product/service development

Kurt Hanks, Larry Belliston & Dave Edwards (1992) *Design yourself!* Menlow Park CA: Crisp Publications.

Bloomsbury Publishing (2003) *Business the ultimate resource.* London UK: Bloomsbury Publishing PLC.

G. Michael Maddock & Luisa C. Uriarte (2011) *Brand new.* Hoboken NJ: John Wiley & Sons.

Alex Osterwalder, Yves Pigneur, Greg Bernarda & Alan Smith (2014) *Value proposition design.* Hoboken NJ: John Wiley & Sons.

Customer service

Jan Carlzon (1989) *Moments of truth.* New York NY: HarperCollins.

Jeffery Gitomer (1998) *Customer satisfaction is worthless, customer loyalty is priceless.* Austin TX: Bard Press.

Geoff Ramm (2015) *Celebrity Service.* Creative Juice Publishing

Operations, process & systems

Mark Graban (2012) *Lean Hospitals 2nd Ed.* Boca Raton, FL: CRC Press

Lee J. Krajewski & Larry P. Ritzman (1996) *Operations Management 4th ed.* Boston MA: Addison-Wesley Publishing Company.

John Seddon (2005) *Freedom from Command and Control.* New York, NY: Productivity Press.

Sales and Marketing

Chet Holmes (2007) *The ultimate sales machine.* New York NY: Penguin Group.

Philip Kotler (1997) *Marketing management 9th Ed.* Upper Saddle River NJ: Prentice-Hall Ltd.

Grant Leboff (2007) *Sales therapy.* Chichester UK: Capstone Publishing Ltd.

Jurgen Wolff (2009) *Marketing for entrepreneurs.* Harlow UK: Pearson Education Limited.

Finance

Clive Marsh (2012) *Financial management for non-financial managers.* London UK: Kogan Page Ltd.

Mike Michalowicz (2014) *Profit first.* Leverkusen DE: budrich Inspirited.

Martin Quinn (2010) *Bookkeeping and accounts for entrepreneurs.* Harlow UK: Pearson Education Limited.

People, leadership and management

John Adair (2002) *The action centred leader.* London UK: The Industrial Society.

Emma Bridger (2015) *Employee engagement.* London UK: Kogan Page Ltd.

Robert B. Cialdini (2007) *Influence.* New York NY: HarperCollins Publishers.

Stephen Covey (1989) *The Seven Habits of Highly Effective People.* New York NY: Simon and Schuster

Peter F. Drucker (1974) *Management.* New York NY: Harper & Row, Publishers.

Kouzes Posner (2002) *The leadership challenge 3rd ed.* San Francisco CA: Jossey-Bass.

Edgar H. Schein (1992) *Organisational culture and leadership 2nd ed.* San Fransisco CA: Jossey-Bass.

James A.F. Stoner, R. Edward Freeman & Daniel R. Gilbert, Jr. (1995) *Management 6th ed.* Englewood Cliffs NJ: Prentice Hall.

Noel M. Tichy (1997) *The leadership engine.* New York NY: HarperCollins Publishers.

Business strategy

Alex Blyth (2009) *How to grow your business for entrepreneurs.* Harlow UK: Pearson Education Limited.

Larry Bossidy & Ram Charan (2002) *Execution.* New York NY: Crown Business.

Keith J. Cunningham (2014) *The ultimate blueprint for an insanely successful business.* Austin TX: Keys to the Vault Publishing.

Michael E. Gerber (2001) *The E myth revisited.* New York NY: HarperCollins Publishers.

Verne Harnish (2014) *Scaling up.* Ashburn VA: Gazelles Inc.

Richard Koch (1999) *Smart things to know about strategy.* Oxford UK: Capstone Publishing.

Alexander Osterwalder & Yves Pigneur (2010) *Business model generation.* Hoboken NJ: John Wiley & Sons.

Michael E. Porter (1985) *Competitive advantage.* New York NY: The Free Press.

Lena Ramfelt, Jonas Kjellberg & Tom Kosnik (2014) *Gear up.* Chichester UK: John Wiley & Sons.

Rodger D. Touchie (1998) *Preparing a successful business plan.* North Vancouver BC: Self-Counsel Press.

Mindset

Maxwell Maltz (1994) *Psycho-cybernetics.* New York NY: Simon & Schuster.

Joseph Murphy revised by Ian McMahan (2000) *The power of your subconscious mind.* New York NY: Reward Books.

Bob Procter (1996) *You were born rich.* Kansas City MO: Praxis International Group.

Expert Contributors

We owe a huge debt of thanks to these expert contributors, for adding their wisdom to the Fine Tuning chapters.

Operations

Chris Clayton, Managing Director, Grey Matters (Europe) Ltd
www.grey-matters.eu

Doug Edworthy, Principle Consultant, Edworthy Management Consultants
www.edworthyconsulting.com

Customer Service

Graham Seymour, previously of Shopper Anonymous
www.shopperanonymous.co.uk

Sales

Clifford Thomas, Managing Director, Business Development Consultancy
www.winmorebusiness.co.uk

Marketing

Emma Pearce, Managing Director, Pearce Marketing
www.pearcemarketing.co.uk

Finance

Shaun Walsh, Managing Partner, Business Growth Services
www.businessgrowthservices.co

Peter Watters, Director, McPhersons Chartered Accountants
www.mcphersons.co.uk

Download the free tools at
www.businessjetengine.co.uk

Contact us at
info@businessjetengine.co.uk